Armies of the Achaemenid Persian Empire, 550–330 BC

Gabriele Esposito is a military historian who works as a freelance author and researcher for some of the most important publishing houses in the military history sector. In particular, he is an expert specializing in uniformology: his interests and expertise range from the ancient civilizations to modern post-colonial conflicts. During recent years, he has conducted and published several researches on the military history of the Latin American countries, with special attention on the War of the Triple Alliance and the War of the Pacific. He is among the leading experts on the military history of the Italian Wars of Unification and the Spanish Carlist Wars. His books and essays are published on a regular basis by Osprey Publishing, Winged Hussar Publishing and Libreria Editrice Goriziana. He is also the author of numerous military history articles appearing in specialized magazines like *Ancient Warfare Magazine*, *Medieval Warfare Magazine*, *The Armourer*, *History of War*, *Guerres et Histoire*, *Focus Storia* and *Focus Storia Wars*.

Armies of the Achaemenid Persian Empire, 550–330 BC

Organization, Weapons and Tactics

Gabriele Esposito

Pen & Sword
MILITARY

First published in Great Britain in 2025 by
Pen & Sword Military
An imprint of Pen & Sword Books Limited
Yorkshire – Philadelphia

ISBN 978 1 03611 287 5

A CIP catalogue record for this book is available from the British Library.

Typeset by Mac Style

MIX
Paper | Supporting responsible forestry
FSC™ C016779

The Publisher's authorised representative in the EU for product safety is Authorised Rep Compliance Ltd., Ground Floor, 71 Lower Baggot Street, Dublin D02 P593, Ireland.
www.arccompliance.com

For a complete list of Pen & Sword titles please contact

PEN & SWORD BOOKS LIMITED
47 Church Street, Barnsley, South Yorkshire, S70 2AS, England
E-mail: enquiries@pen-and-sword.co.uk
Website: www.pen-and-sword.co.uk
or
PEN AND SWORD BOOKS
1950 Lawrence Road, Havertown, PA 19083, USA
E-mail: uspen-and-sword@casematepublishers.com
Website: www.penandswordbooks.com

Contents

Acknowledgements

This book is dedicated to my magnificent parents, Maria Rosaria and Benedetto, for the immense love and fundamental support that they always give me. It is thanks to their precious advice deriving from long experience that the present book is much better than planned. A very special thanks goes to Philip Sidnell, the commissioning editor of my books for Pen & Sword: his love for history and his passion for publishing are the key factors behind the success of our publications. Many thanks also to the production manager of this title, Matt Jones, for his excellent work and great enthusiasm. A special mention is due to Tony Walton for the magnificent work of editing that he makes for all my books. A very special mention goes to the brilliant re-enactment groups that collaborated with their photographs to the creation of this book: without the incredible work of research of their members, the final result of this publication would not have been the same. As a result, I want to express my deep gratitude to the following living history associations: Somatophylaques and Make Carthage Great Again from France, Koryvantes from Greece, Ancient Thrace from Bulgaria, Amages Drachen from Germany and Scythian State from Ukraine. A very special thanks goes to Patricio Greve Moller, one of the greatest South American military historians of the present times, for having painted fifty of the magnificent costumes reproduced in this book. Patricio is a brilliant historian but also a talented illustrator, whose detailed and colourful art has brought back to life many warriors who had never been reconstructed before in a graphic way.

Introduction

The main aim of this book is to present a detailed overview of the history, organization, equipment and tactics of the military forces deployed by Achaemenid Persia during the period 550–330 BC. The Achaemenid Empire founded by Cyrus the Great was one of the major military powers of Antiquity, extending over a large portion of the known Mediterranean and Middle Eastern world. It comprised territories located in three continents (Asia, Africa and Europe) and was inhabited by a multitude of different peoples. From a cultural and social point of view, the Persian Empire was without doubt the most multi-ethnic state of Antiquity: the Achaemenid 'Kings of Kings' ruled over present-day Iran as well as Mesopotamia and Egypt. These regions, during the centuries that preceded the ascendancy of the Persians, had seen the emergence of great civilizations that had shaped the development of humanity. The Achaemenids also controlled Anatolia (which was inhabited by several different peoples) and other rich areas of the Levant such as Phoenicia and Judaea. It is important to note that the Persians also had a strong presence in Central Asia, where they ruled over the wild territories of Bactria and Sogdia (from which they even expanded into northern India, corresponding to modern-day Pakistan). The frontiers of such a large and multi-cultural empire were highly flexible, as the Achaemenids continued to expand their domains long after the end of Cyrus the Great's reign. The Persians came to exert their political influence over Ethiopia and Nubia in Africa, Oman in the Arabian Peninsula, the Caucasus in Asia and even conquered – albeit for a short period – some significant territories in Europe. As we will see in the following pages, they campaigned in present-day Ukraine and occupied Thrace (modern Bulgaria), while for a few years they also transformed the Kingdom of Macedonia into one of their vassal states. All these political successes were made possible by the massive military resources deployed by the Achaemenids, which were forged by Cyrus the Great. Cyrus made two fundamental contributions to the creation of the empire: first, he transformed the Persians from a series of autonomous tribal groups into a unified people; second, he took control – in a relatively peaceful way – of the empire that the Medes had created following the fall of the Assyrian Empire. As we will see, the Achaemenid Empire was ruled jointly by the Persians and the Medes, two peoples having many cultural elements in common, who had migrated to Iran several centuries before the ascendancy of Cyrus the Great (who was half-Persian and half-Median). Following their unification, the Persians and the Medes were able to launch their conquest of the known world. This seemed impossible to arrest until they decided to invade Greece, initiating the Greco-Persian Wars. These conflicts changed forever the history of the Achaemenid Empire, revealing that the Persian military forces could be defeated by just a few Greek cities. The many setbacks suffered by the Achaemenids during the Greco-Persian Wars led to the end of Persian expansionism and the beginning of a long phase of consolidation for the Achaemenid Empire. This was characterized by the outbreak of civil wars within its territories and the temporary secession of some areas (such as Egypt). Despite experiencing many difficulties, the Achaemenids were able to preserve the integrity of their empire until the Macedonians – guided by Alexander the Great – launched their spectacular invasion of Persian lands. By 330 BC, the Achaemenid Empire, after more than two centuries, came tumbling down and a new world was born, one in which the Hellenic culture exported by the pikes of Alexander's phalangites would play a prominent role. In this book, we will outline all the major military campaigns fought by the Persians, from the days of Cyrus the Great to the fall of the Achaemenid Empire. We will also detail the organization, equipment and tactics of the many different contingents that made up the Persian armies: the famous royal guard of the Immortals, the Persians and the Medes, as well as the Kissians, Babylonians, Assyrians, Phoenicians, Jews, Arabs, Armenians, Cappadocians, Paphlagonians, Cilicians, Lycians, Carians, Phrygians, Lydians, Scythians, Sogdians, Bactrians, Thracians, Greeks, Egyptians, Nubians, Ethiopians, Libyans and Indians. Each contingent will be covered in detail in order to provide a complete description of the Achaemenid army's complex structure.

Chapter 1

The Rise of Cyrus the Great

The ancient Persians were a nomadic Iranian people who settled in present-day south-western Iran around 1000 BC. They comprised several warlike tribes whose members lived in a pastoral manner, following their migrating herds of sheep and goats. The homeland of the Persians was in the Zagros Mountains, where they settled alongside the native Elamites. Before the arrival of the Persians, the Elamites had always played an important role in the politics of Mesopotamia, despite being less powerful than the peoples living around them. According to the latest research, the Persians migrated to south-western Iran from the Caucasus region, in search of better pastures for their herds and probably wanting to settle down in a region that was not inhabited by other nomadic peoples. The Elamites lived in the southern portion of Iraq and in present-day Kuwait. The Persians established their new homeland east of the main Elamite territories, in the current Iranian province of Fars. After they had settled in this region, it became known as Persis. It was in this area of south-western Iran that the Persians built their first major urban centres of Persepolis and Pasargadae as they gradually transformed themselves from nomad to sedentary communities. The Persians were not the only pastoral nomadic people to enter the territory of Iran during the eleventh century BC, the Medes, who had a lot in common with the Persians, having migrated across the Middle East before settling in north-western Iran. The new homeland of the Medes was located just north of the Elamite territories, in an area that is today partly crossed by the border that divides Iraq from Iran. The Medes were initially stronger and more numerous than the Persians. They established their capital at Ecbatana and soon started to carry out an expansionist policy, which threatened the Elamites and their main urban centre of Susa. The Medes, like the Persians, consisted of several different pastoral tribes. However, they were much more warlike than the sedentary peoples living around them, conducting a series of successful military campaigns that resulted in their progressive expansion.

The migrations of the Persians and the Medes coincided with a power vacuum in the Middle East, caused by the progressive decline of the Assyrian Empire. The Assyrians had dominated the region of Mesopotamia for many decades thanks to the strength of their armies and superior military tactics. When the Assyrians weakened

Map showing the maximum territorial extent of the Achaemenid Empire and its administrative subdivision into twenty satrapies or provinces.
(CC BY 4.0, Wikimedia User 'Cattette')

Persian cavalry officer wearing a magnificent example of golden scale armour. Note the decorations of the sword's scabbard and the quiver. Offensive weapons include a sword, bow, akinakes dagger and war hammer. (*Colour plate by Patricio Greve Moller, copyright of Gabriele Esposito*)

due to a series of internal issues, the Persians and the Medes took advantage of the changing situation and entered the territory of Iran from the Caucasus. The Babylonians, who dominated the southern portion of Mesopotamia, benefitted from the decline of the Assyrians, who had long been their main rivals. However, the Babylonians could do little to prevent the settling of the Persians and the Medes around the Elamite territories. Over time, despite some periods of Assyrian revival, the newcomers consolidated their presence in Iran and became increasingly strong. The Assyrians were able to exert their dominance over the Medes for some time, obliging them to pay an annual tribute. By 620 BC, however, the earlier unity of the Assyrian Empire had almost disappeared and many vassal states had started to rebel against their overlords. The Medes were one of these states, ceasing to pay their tributes to the collapsing Assyrian Empire and formed a strong military alliance with the Babylonians. Between 616 and 609 BC, the Medes and the Babylonians attacked the Assyrian heartland, devastating large swathes of Mesopotamia. In 612 BC, they captured the Assyrian capital of Nineveh, an event that was a real turning point in the history of the ancient Middle East. Following the destruction of the Assyrian Empire, the Medes established their own unified kingdom in Iran and started to expand very rapidly. They conquered most of Assyria and reached the borders of Anatolia, creating a mighty empire that had significant military resources. With the fall of Nineveh, four major powers emerged in the Middle East: the Median Kingdom, the Neo-Babylonian Empire (which dominated southern Mesopotamia), the Kingdom of Lydia (which controlled Anatolia) and Egypt (which regained independence after having been occupied by the Assyrians). After the establishment of the Median Kingdom, the Persians became vassals of the Medes as they were militarily much weaker. With the progress of time, however, an ambitious and powerful aristocratic family emerged among the Persians. Known as the Achaemenids, they transformed the Persian tribes into a major regional power.

The Achaemenids were initially rulers of the city of Anshan, which was located not far from the Elamite capital of Susa. Their name derived from their family's mythical founder, Achaemenes. During the late seventh century BC, Astyages, the supreme ruler of the Median Kingdom, decided to cement his alliance with the Persians by marrying his daughter, Mandane, to the King of Anshan, Cambyses I. The leading figure of the Achaemenid family, Cambyses had ambitions to unite all the Persian tribes under his personal rule. The union between Mandane and Cambyses produced an heir named Cyrus, who would become one of Antiquity's most important historical figures. The young Cyrus inherited the Achaemenid throne following his father's death. Like his father, however, Cyrus ruled as a vassal of his grandfather, Astyages, and not as an independent king. Cyrus, however, was extremely ambitious

Persian infantry officer wearing a cuirass made of leather and bronze scales. The practice of wearing animal skins (mostly of lions, tigers and leopards) distinguished officers and standard-bearers from common soldiers. The piece of cloth attached to the bottom part of the shield was designed to protect the legs from enemy arrows. (*Colour plate by Patricio Greve Moller, copyright of Gabriele Esposito*)

and wanted to become the sole master of Iran. He gradually unified all the Persian communities under his rule by completing a process of urbanization that was already taking place in Persis. He established his royal capital at Pasargadae and started assembling significant military forces. In 553 BC, six years after ascending to the throne, he revolted against his grandfather. Astyages sent his army against the Persians, under the leadership of Harpagus, who was one of the most experienced Median military commanders. Harpagus, however, defected with a significant portion of his army and joined Cyrus in the war against the Medes. This gave Cyrus the upper hand and enabled him to defeat the remaining loyal Medes within just three years. In 550 BC, the Persians captured Ecbatana and obtained a decisive victory over the Medes. Astyages was turned over to Cyrus by his own dissatisfied nobles, but was spared by his grandson. Cyrus, being half-Persian and half-Median, was able to unify the two Iranian peoples into a single state that soon acquired the dimensions of an empire. The Medes were not submitted by the Persians, retaining a prominent position in the new state created by Cyrus. In both honour and war, they stood next to the Persians, and their court ceremony was adopted by the new Achaemenid sovereigns. The Achaemenid

Persian officer of the Immortals, wearing ceremonial court dress. Note the rich decorations embroidered on his tunic and overcoat. (*Colour plate by Patricio Greve Moller, copyright of Gabriele Esposito*)

kings, starting with Cyrus, spent the summer months in the former Median capital of Ecbatana. The extensive new domain created by Cyrus was a true Persian-Median Empire, being ruled by Persians and Medes who enjoyed the same social status.

Cyrus spent the early years of his reign fighting in north-eastern Iran and Central Asia in an attempt to pacify the regions of Sogdia and Bactria. These were inhabited by nomadic peoples of the Eurasian steppes who had previously acknowledged Median supremacy but were now revolting against the Achaemenids. Cyrus subdued the rebels in Sogdia and Bactria in a series of military campaigns and also fought against the Scythians (who were called the Saka by the Persians). The Scythians were a major military power of Asia, controlling an immense territory stretching from the Caspian Sea to the Caucasus. After securing his frontier in Central Asia, Cyrus turned his attention westwards and decided to invade the rich Kingdom of Lydia, which was ruled by a very capable monarch, Croesus. Lydia, during the years that followed the fall of the Assyrian Empire, had expanded very rapidly and come to control most of Anatolia. Under the leadership of Croesus, the Lydians had submitted the Thracian tribes living in the region of Phrygia (which had their capital at Gordion), as well as the Greek colonies located on the coastline of Asia Minor. Croesus established positive relations with the ruling elites of all the peoples he submitted and never imposed a strict centralized control over his client kings. Through his conquests, the Kingdom of Lydia flourished economically, connecting Greece with the Middle East. Croesus annexed to his domains several regions that were rich in important natural resources, including Caria, Mysia, Paphlagonia and Bithynia. Only some small areas of Anatolia – notably Lycia and Cilicia – were not submitted by the Lydian monarch, who became extremely rich in just a few years and established positive diplomatic relations with both the Medes and the major Greek cities. Following Cyrus's ascendancy to the throne of Media, Croesus became increasingly worried about the expansionist ambitions of the Persians and prepared for war. According to the great ancient historian Herodotus, Croesus consulted the Oracle of Delphi in Greece before deciding what to do about the Persians. The Oracle told him that he would destroy a great empire by attacking Cyrus. Croesus interpreted this response as a positive omen for his offensive plans, and thus decided to launch an attack in 547 BC. What he did not know was that he would end up destroying his own 'great empire', not that of Cyrus.

Croesus allied himself with Egypt and the Babylonians before attacking Persian lands in Cappadocia. During the ensuing conflict, however, he received very little help from his allies, who avoided any direct confrontation with the Persians. Cyrus responded very rapidly to the Lydian offensive, marching with his forces to face Croesus. The first major clash of the campaign took place at Pteria and ended with a partial defeat for the Lydians. Croesus escaped from the battlefield with some of his troops and went to his fortified capital of Sardis, where he prepared for a further pitched battle. This encounter came at Thymbra and was another defeat for the Lydians. After having routed the Croesus, the Persians attacked the fortified city of Sardis and eventually captured it after a difficult siege. The fall of its capital in 546 BC marked the end of the Kingdom of Lydia, which was annexed to the expanding domains of the Persians. Croesus, however, was not killed by Cyrus, instead becoming one of his most trusted advisors. After having gained control over Lydia's impressive treasury, Cyrus could finance more military campaigns of conquest. He sent Harpagus to the coastline of Asia Minor in order to force the local Greek colonies to recognize the political supremacy of the Achaemenids. The Persians also completed the conquest of Anatolia, occupying Lycia and Cilicia. Cyrus's armies then entered the rich region of Phoenicia from the north. While relatively small, Phoenicia was characterized by several flourishing port cities, such as Tyre and Sidon, that exerted their naval and commercial dominance over much of the Mediterranean Sea. The multinational empire that Cyrus was building did not have an outlet to the Mediterranean, but by submitting the Phoenician cities with their large military and commercial fleets the Persians would be able to create their own naval forces. Conquering the Phoenician coastal centres was not an easy task for the Persians, who had to besiege and storm several of them by building earthworks to breach the walls. By 542 BC, however, the Achaemenid conquest of Phoenicia had been completed.

During the years 542–540 BC, Cyrus invaded the territories of the Elamites and conquered their capital of Susa. This represented a clear threat to the Babylonians' dominance over southern Mesopotamia and was perceived as a direct provocation in Babylon. As a result, in 539 BC, hostilities broke out between the Persians and the Babylonians. The Neo-Babylonian Empire was at that time one of the greatest in Antiquity, extending over most of Iraq and other areas of the Levant such as Syria or Judea. After the fall of Nineveh, the Babylonians had conquered the richest regions of the former Assyrian Empire and had tried to limit as much as possible the expansionism of their former Median allies. When Cyrus attacked the Babylonians, his enemies mobilized all their forces and moved against the Persians at the city of Opis, located on the Tigris River, north of Babylon. The Battle of Opis was one of the largest clashes fought during Antiquity, with the participation of many thousands of warriors. The Babylonians were soundly defeated and were forced to fall back on their capital. At this point, some of the defeated commanders started negotiating with Cyrus, eager to avoid a Persian siege of Babylon. The city was crowded with civilians, and thus an Achaemenid attack could potentially result in a massacre. The Persians, by using a basin dug earlier by the Babylonians, diverted the Euphrates

Persian Immortal wearing ceremonial court dress, which for Persian guardsmen included a long tunic with rich decorative embroidering. (*Colour plate by Patricio Greve Moller, copyright of Gabriele Esposito*)

River so that the water level dropped and allowed them to march directly through the river bed to enter the city at night. The defenders of Babylon surrendered without a fight and Cyrus entered the great capital in triumph. With the fall of Babylon, the echoes of which resounded outside the Middle East, the Achaemenids could annex to their domains all the regions that had previously been part of the Neo-Babylonian Empire, including Syria and Judea. Cyrus, after proclaiming himself 'King of the Four Corners of the World', acted according to his usual political practices: he established strong alliances with the ruling classes of the territories that he had conquered and granted freedom to many of the recently submitted peoples. The Achaemenid monarch also repatriated displaced peoples (like the Hebrews who lived as exiles in Babylon) and restored the temples of all religions.

By 540 BC, the warlike steppe people of the Massagetae controlled a sizeable portion of territory east of the Caspian Sea. The great military resources of the Massagetae were too powerful for the Scythians, who were forced to abandon their traditional homeland in Inner Asia due to the expansionist pressure exerted by their neighbours.

Median Immortal wearing ceremonial court dress, which for Median guardsmen include the peculiar headgear shown here and trousers. (*Colour plate by Patricio Greve Moller, copyright of Gabriele Esposito*)

The Scythians crossed much of southern Russia before entering Ukraine, a region of Europe that contained all the necessary conditions for creating a new Scythian homeland. Southern Ukraine had vast plains, where pastures for the horses were abundant, and was rich in water supplies. It was thus perfect for a nomadic people like the Scythians who considered horses as the most important of their properties. Having defeated the Scythians, the Massagetae became an important military power and started to represent a menace for the emerging empire of Cyrus. Initially, Cyrus tried to avoid a direct confrontation with the nomads, being well aware of their great fighting capabilities. Indeed, he offered a peace treaty to them and proposed to marry the queen of the Massagetae. Cyrus's offers, however, were turned down by the Massagetae, who thereafter started to attack the north-eastern territories of the Achaemenid Empire. Cyrus responded by launching an invasion of Massagetae lands around 530 BC, advancing towards the Jaxartes River at the head of a large army. The Massagetae employed elusive tactics similar to those of the Scythians and other steppe peoples of the time. As a result, the Persians of Cyrus found it very difficult to intercept them and force them to fight in a pitched battle. Hoping to trick his enemies, Cyrus left behind a small portion of his invading army in an isolated position. The Massagetae, seeing the opportunity to obtain a clear victory, attacked the small Persian contingent. Before this force could be destroyed, however, Cyrus arrived on the battlefield at the head of the rest of his army and soundly defeated the Massagetae. Nevertheless, the Massagetae did not surrender after this setback, continuing to provoke the invading Persian forces. After assembling another massive army, they challenged Cyrus on the open field. During the ensuing battle – one of the largest ever fought in the Eurasian steppes – the Persians were defeated due to the numerical superiority of their enemy. According to Herodotus's description of this clash, Cyrus was killed in combat by the Massagetae. After decades of victorious campaigns, the founder of the Persian Empire – who soon became known as Cyrus the Great – had died while fighting a secondary campaign in an obscure corner of his immense domains.

Persian Immortal equipped with scale armour and rectangular body shield. (*Colour plate by Patricio Greve Moller, copyright of Gabriele Esposito*)

Persian Immortal armed with thrusting spear, throwing spear and axe.
His shield is decorated with incisions and is covered with leopard skin on the outer surface.
(*Colour plate by Patricio Greve Moller, copyright of Gabriele Esposito*)

Chapter 2

The Expansion of the Persian Empire

Cyrus the Great was succeeded by his eldest son, Cambyses II, who came to rule over a vast but young empire that had just one rival in the Middle East: Egypt. Before his sudden death, Cyrus had planned to invade Egypt, and this project was continued by his ambitious son, who was determined to unite all the richest lands of the known world under his rule. At that time Egypt was ruled by Pharaoh Amasis II, a member of the Twenty-sixth Dynasty that had freed Egypt from foreign occupation. Having been invaded by the Assyrians, Egypt was briefly dominated by the Neo-Babylonian Empire until the latter was defeated by the Egyptians at the Battle of Carchemish in 605 BC. The rulers of the Twenty-sixth Dynasty secured the independence of their homeland thanks to support from the Kingdom of Lydia, which provided them with substantial numbers of Greek mercenaries. Equipped as fully armoured hoplites, the Greek fighters were superior to any local infantry force deployed in the Middle East and played a crucial role in securing Egypt's independence. Following the fall of the Kingdom of Lydia, Amasis II allied himself with Polycrates, the tyrant ruler of Samos in Greece. The pharaohs of the Twenty-sixth Dynasty were totally dependent upon foreign mercenaries to defend their realm and needed a constant flow of 'men of bronze' (i.e. hoplites) from Greece. In 526 BC, shortly before the Persian invasion of Egypt, Amasis II died and was succeeded by Psamtik III. The new ruler was young and had no military experience, and he was soon abandoned by Polycrates of Samos, who wanted to avoid a confrontation with the Persians. Cambyses's military forces, counting on the support of the Arab tribes living on Egypt's eastern border, rapidly crossed the Sinai Desert and confronted the enemy forces at Pelusium during the spring of 525 BC. Shortly before the Battle of Pelusium, the many Greek mercenaries in Egyptian service, commanded by Phanes of Halicarnassus (a Carian military leader), abandoned Psamtik III, who was subsequently soundly defeated by Cambyses. The pharaoh fell back with his surviving troops to Memphis, where he organized a last desperate defence. The Egyptian capital was besieged by the Persians and – despite the heroic behaviour of its defenders – finally fell after a long siege. Psamtik III was captured and then executed by the Persians, who thereafter rapidly completed their conquest of Egypt.

Persian Immortal equipped with a corselet of scale armour. His offensive weapons – as happened quite frequently for Achaemenid foot troops – include both a spear and a bow. (*Colour plate by Patricio Greve Moller, copyright of Gabriele Esposito*)

Persian *sparabara* infantryman equipped with a rectangular body shield and a cuirass of padded armour.
(*Colour plate by Patricio Greve Moller, copyright of Gabriele Esposito*)

The seizing of Egyptian lands had a series of important consequences for the Persian Empire. First of all, it enabled the Achaemenids to occupy more territories that had previously been part of the Egyptian sphere of influence, including Cyprus and the eastern portion of Libya. The latter was inhabited by a series of warlike tribes but also by large numbers of Greeks, who had established two flourishing colonies at Cyrene and Barca. Cambyses respected the political freedoms of his new Greek subjects and followed a similar strategy with the Kingdom of Kush, a realm extending over most of Nubia (present-day Sudan) whose history had long been linked with that of Egypt. Cambyses also established positive relations with the Arabs who controlled the stretch of desert between Gaza and the Egyptian frontier. The warlike Arabs, who had fought for centuries against the Assyrians and the Babylonians, provided the Persians with water during the difficult crossing of the Sinai and thus were fundamental for Cambyses's success over Psamtik III. The Persians, thanks to their conquest of Egypt, greatly enlarged their naval forces by absorbing Egyptian vessels into their fleet, and also started playing a prominent political role in the Red Sea. They conducted a minor military campaign in northern Ethiopia – which was only partially successful – and established indirect control over parts of modern Oman in the Persian Gulf. Cambyses had himself proclaimed Pharaoh of Upper and Lower Egypt, but did not act in the usual Achaemenid manner towards his new Egyptian subjects: he did not show respect for the traditional religious rites of the Egyptians (for example by spoiling the riches of many important temples) and failed to establish a political alliance with the Egyptian aristocracy. This caused widespread malcontent in the land of the pharaohs, whose population always perceived the Persian newcomers as brutal usurpers who showed no respect for their religion. Cambyses died childless in 522 BC and was succeeded by his younger brother, Bardiya, who ruled over the Persian Empire for only a few months until he was murdered by the future Darius I, who succeeded him.

Darius came from a secondary branch of the Achaemenid family and was the son of Hystaspes, who had been nominated governor of Persis and Bactria during the late reign of Cyrus the Great. Darius fought under the orders of Cambyses during the campaign for the conquest of Egypt, and thus was an experienced military commander. Like his predecessors, he had great political ambitions and wanted to continue the expansion of the Achaemenid Empire. In the early phase of his reign, he had to face a series of revolts organized across his domains by the supporters of Bardiya. These were particularly strong in Elam and Babylonia, but Darius was eventually able to restore order inside his empire thanks to the decisive support of his armies, which remained loyal to him. In 516 BC, having secured his position as supreme monarch, Darius embarked on a campaign in Central Asia with the objective

Kissian *sparabara* infantryman equipped with a rectangular body shield and a cuirass that comprises some elements made of bronze. (*Colour plate by Patricio Greve Moller, copyright of Gabriele Esposito*)

Persian *sparabara* infantryman. His rectangular body shield is mostly made of wicker.
(*Colour plate by Benedetto Esposito, copyright of Gabriele Esposito*)

of establishing firm control over Bactria before penetrating the Indus Valley from the north. In 535 BC, Cyrus the Great had conducted a foray into northern India, and Darius wanted to follow the example of his illustrious predecessor. He marched into present-day Afghanistan and reached the region of Taxila in modern Pakistan, before quartering in Gandhara during the winter. The Persians then entered the Indus Valley in the spring of 515 BC and conquered much of the region by defeating the local rulers. Most of these tribal leaders were forced to become vassals of the Achaemenids, which allowed a stable Persian presence to be established in northern India. According to ancient sources, Darius came to control all the lands surrounding the Indus River from Gandhara to present-day Karachi. No other Middle Eastern monarch had ever conquered parts of India, meaning Darius's achievements were of great historical importance.

By 515 BC, the military expansion of the Persians had pushed the Achaemenid Empire to the borders of Scythian territory in the Caucasus. The Persians, well aware of the great military capabilities of the Scythians, considered them dangerous potential enemies. Darius planned to transform the Black Sea into a 'Persian lake', to do which he had no alternative but to invade the Scythian lands of southern Ukraine. Once in that region, the Persians would have been able to occupy Crimea and gain access to all the rich natural resources of the Scythians. Around 515 BC, Darius sent a small naval expedition, consisting of thirty warships commanded by the satrap of Cappadocia, to the northern shore of the Black Sea. The Persians explored the area and conducted a series of devastating raids, which resulted in the capture of many Scythians who were later transported to Persia as slaves. The positive results achieved by this minor naval expedition convinced Darius that an invasion of Ukraine was possible. However, instead of attacking Scythian lands from the east, by moving north of the Caucasus Mountains, the Persians decided to cross the Black Sea at the Bosporus Strait by building an enormous bridge of boats. They did so for two main reasons: first, because crossing the Caucasus with a large army was at the time an incredibly difficult if not impossible task; second, because by building a bridge of boats to cross the Bosporus, they would shock the Greeks and have established a strategic infrastructure that would be fundamental for any future invasion of Greece. To reach the Scythian lands, which were located north of the Danube River, the Persians were obliged to cross the southern portion of the eastern Balkans that was inhabited by the Thracians. In 513 BC, after completing the preparation of his troops, Darius crossed into Europe and started ravaging Thrace. He met no strong resistance from the Thracian tribes, who were keen to avoid any direct confrontation with the Persians. The Thracian leaders soon understood that the Achaemenid troops had come to the Balkans to attack the Scythians north of the Danube and not to occupy their lands. To avoid any problems, several Thracian chieftains formally agreed to submit to the Persians, believing that this would have no future consequences for them. Other Thracian warlords instead harassed the marching Persians by launching surprise attacks with hit-and-run light infantry tactics. These caused significant losses to Darius's troops, but could not stop the Persian advance. After crossing the Danube practically unopposed, the Persians entered Scythian territory. At this point, the king of the Scythians, Idanthyrsus, summoned the leaders of all the peoples living around his realm to a meeting during which the monarchs of the northern Balkans decided how to deal with the Achaemenid invasion. Idanthyrsus wanted to form a large anti-Persian alliance, but the meeting was a political failure, with both the Agathyrsi and the Tauri refusing to support the Scythians in the war against Darius. During the previous decades, the Scythians had expanded across south-western Ukraine and reached the Danube, depriving the Agathyrsi of most of their lands, so it was understandable that they sided with the Persians in the hope of regaining their recently lost territories. The decision of the Tauri was also quite logical, as the Scythians were at that time common enemies of the Persians and the Tauri.

Facing a massive invasion and having no allies, Idanthyrsus mobilized all his forces and started to fight the enemy in the traditional way of the Eurasian steppes, avoiding any direct confrontation with the invaders and employing a scorched earth strategy. The Scythians evaded the pursuing Persians using feints and retreated eastwards across the Pontic Steppe, attacking the invaders with hit-and-run guerrilla tactics. They devastated the countryside that had to be crossed by the Persians, blocked wells, intercepted convoys in the rear of the enemy, destroyed pastures and ambushed isolated Achaemenid contingents. The invaders soon started to experience serious difficulties, being unused to fight in the steppe. They began running out of supplies and clean water, while pursuing an enemy who vanished every time they tried to intercept them. The Scythians had no urban settlements where the Persians could stop and establish a base. Furthermore, they had perfect knowledge of their home territory, while the Achaemenid troops had no idea where the enemy could hide. According to ancient writers, becoming highly frustrated, Darius I sent a letter to Idanthyrsus in which he accused him of being a coward who lacked the courage to fight against the Persians. Idanthyrsus responded that he was just waging war in his own traditional way, like the Scythians had done for centuries. Time and space were important factors that worked in favour of the Scythians, since Darius could not spend too many months away from his empire to campaign in the Pontic Steppe. The Persian invading force only survived thanks to the supplies transported across the Black Sea by the Achaemenid navy. Nevertheless, after several weeks of fruitless marching across southern Ukraine, Darius was obliged to suspend the advance of his

Persian *sparabara* infantryman wearing a pointed helmet made of bronze. (*Photo and copyright by Somatophylaques*)

troops. The Persians reached the banks of the Volga River and built eight forts in the area before starting their return journey. The forts, garrisoned by Achaemenid soldiers, were presumably destroyed by the Scythians soon after Darius went away. The Persian retreat across the eastern Balkans was a long and difficult one, the Achaemenid troops often coming under attacked from Thracian tribes during their

Persian *sparabara* infantryman wearing a light cuirass made of linen.
(*Photo and copyright by Somatophylaques*)

march. Before returning to Asia Minor, Darius formally organized Thrace as a new satrapy known as Skudra, which he intended to use as a bridgehead for a future invasion of Greece. As soon as the bulk of the Achaemenid troops had left the region, however, most of the Thracian tribes rose up in revolt and initiated skirmishes with the tiny military garrisons that the Persians had left behind in the Balkans. The Persian invasion of Scythia had been a total failure for Darius, but it had also caused serious problems to the Scythians, who had ravaged some of the most fertile areas of their homeland.

Darius I conducted many military campaigns and was the initiator of the Greco-Persian Wars, as we will see in the next chapter. However, he also gave the Achaemenid Empire a strong and effective administrative organization. He structured his domains on twenty provinces known as satrapies, each of which was ruled by a satrap, or governor, who was appointed by the monarch. Each satrapy, according to its demographical capabilities and territorial extent, had to pay a certain amount of taxes and provide a particular number of warriors or warships for the formation of the Persian army and navy. Most of the satraps were Persians or Medes and came from the Achaemenid royal house or from the six major aristocratic families of the empire's nobility. Each governor had a secretary, who was tasked with controlling the actions of his satrap and with reporting any infraction to the king he committed. Royal inspectors, appointed by the monarch, were constantly on the move across the empire in order to check that the finances and military resources of each province were in good order. Aramaic was chosen as the official language of the Achaemenid administration, and a 'Royal Road' – a sort of imperial highway – was built during Darius's reign to connect Sardis in the west with Susa in the east. The Royal Road was mostly used by the mounted couriers of the king, who could travel the immense distance separating Sardis from Susa (1,677 miles) in just nine days to transmit orders from the Achaemenid court. The construction of the Royal Road and of other elements of infrastructure greatly helped the flourishing of commerce in the Persian domains, meaning that tradesmen could move freely and safely across the whole Middle East in order to sell or buy goods originating from every corner of the Achaemenid Empire.

Chapter 3

The Greco-Persian Wars

Since the eighth century BC, the western coast of Asia Minor had been progressively colonized by the Greeks, who created several new *poleis* in the region. These were assembled into two large communities, that of Aeolia and Ionia. Until 546 BC, the Greek cities of Asia Minor flourished largely undisturbed, not being menaced by any bordering country. The internal part of Anatolia was controlled by the Kingdom of Lydia, which had quite positive relations with the Greeks. The Greeks were fully independent and only had to pay a yearly tribute in gold to Lydia. Once Cyrus the Great conquered the Kingdom of Lydia, the Greeks of Aeolia and Ionia bordered with a gigantic empire that had no intention of preserving their previous privileges and liberties. Cyrus soon organized an expedition against the Greek cities of Asia Minor, led by his Median general Harpagus. Although Harpagus was able to subdue the *poleis* of western Anatolia after only a brief campaign, the Greeks had no intention of giving up the fight. They proved very difficult to rule for the Persians, refusing to pay taxes and always being ready to rise up in open revolt. In most areas of their growing empire, including in Lydia, the Persians had always formed an alliance with the various local aristocracies after defeating them, but such a political operation proved impossible for the Greek cities of Asia Minor, where all citizens had more or less the same rights and social position. For the first time, the Persians were dealing with a people made up of free individuals rather than subjects used to serving under a supreme monarch. The Achaemenids backed the ascendancy of tyrants in several *poleis*, but this was not enough to secure their control over Asia Minor. Most of their allied tyrants were soon killed or expelled by popular revolts of their citizens. Most of the Greeks from Asia were sure that their mainland 'brothers' would help them against the foreign invader, since by the beginning of the fifth century BC western Anatolia was widely considered as an organic part of the Greek world. The Persians were well aware of this, but had plans to continue their expansion towards Greece in the future. As a result, they tried to form a network of alliances with some cities of mainland Greece.

Persian *takabara* infantryman carrying a crescent-shaped shield and axe.
(*Colour plate by Patricio Greve Moller, copyright of Gabriele Esposito*)

Persian *takabara* infantryman carrying a crescent-shaped shield and spear.
(*Photo and copyright by Petar Chapkanov of Ancient Thrace*)

In 499 BC, a first military expedition was mounted against the Greek island of Naxos. This was organized by one of the tyrants loyal to Persia, Aristagoras of Miletus, but saw the participation of a sizeable Persian force. The attack against Naxos, however, ended in failure: after four months of siege, the Persians abandoned the island, having suffered severe economic losses. They had underestimated the military capabilities of the Greeks and had shown their own martial weakness. Consequently, before they could plan any further expansionist expedition, their former Milesian allies, guided by Aristagoras, rose up in rebellion. This was the beginning of the Ionian Revolt, a conflict that would change forever the relations between the Greek world and the Persians. Several Greek cities of Asia Minor had already assembled fighting contingents in Myus, in order to support the Persian efforts against Naxos. However, when news of the Milesian revolt reached Myus, the Greek soldiers mutinied and joined the rebellion. Aristagoras presented himself as the leader of the Asian Greeks in the upcoming struggle against the Achaemenids and ordered the arrest of most of the other tyrants, and most of the Asian *poleis* were thus rapidly freed from indirect Persian control and transformed instead into democracies. Aristagoras was even able to capture the large fleet that the Persians had assembled to attack Naxos, meaning the Achaemenids found themselves with no naval forces in the Aegean. The tyrants installed by the Persians had not been able to control the situation: differently from those of mainland Greece, they were not popular leaders with great personal abilities, just loyal officers who ruled on behalf of their Achaemenid masters. In the winter of 499 BC, in view of an anticipated Persian counter-attack by land and sea, Aristagoras went to mainland Greece in search of allies. Aristagoras tried to create an alliance with the Spartans, but they rejected his offer. He then went to Athens, a city that was already hostile to the Persians. Darius had previously favoured the ascendancy of a pro-Persian tyrant in Athens named Hippias, but he had been expelled from the city by the Athenians, who established a new democratic regime.

Having been removed as tyrant of Athens, Hippias became a member of the Achaemenid court and was able to gain the support of his new protectors. As a result, in the years preceding the outbreak of the Ionian Revolt, the Persians had ordered the Athenians to accept Hippias back as their tyrant. Athens obviously refused, and from that moment on the city considered itself at war against the Persian Empire. Aristagoras, aware of this antagonism towards the Achaemenids, was able to gain unconditional support for the revolt from the Athenians. The city of Athens, with its new form of democracy, had been a model for the *poleis* of Asia Minor in their struggle against tyrants imposed by the foreign conquerors. Furthermore, Athens was an Ionian city, like most of those that were now rebelling. The city of Eretria also agreed to help Aristagoras, probably in exchange for the support received from Miletus during a previous war. The Athenians sent a total of twenty trireme warships to Asia Minor, while the Eretrians dispatched a smaller contingent of just five triremes. The Greek army of Asia Minor, reinforced by the Athenians and Eretrians, assembled at Ephesus and then marched against Sardis, the capital of the Persian province of Lydia in the heart of Anatolia. The Persians, taken aback by this aggressive move, were unable to mount a proper defence of the city. After a brief assault, the Greeks conquered Sardis. The Persian garrison of the city, however, was not destroyed: under the command of Artaphernes, it still resisted in the citadel. At some point, for unknown reasons, the lower city set on fire, obliging the Persians to come out from the citadel in order to avoid being caught up in the conflagration. Against all odds, their desperate counter-attack was successful, causing the Greeks to retreat from Sardis. Nevertheless, most of the city was destroyed by the flames. After this episode, the Persians realized that the revolt was a serious affair and thus started to assemble a large army with which to crush it. Meanwhile, the demoralized Greeks returned to Ephesus. Artaphernes organized a large cavalry force in central Anatolia, with which he was able to intercept the retreating Greeks on the outskirts of Ephesus. During the ensuing battle, the Greek army was completely routed, suffering many casualties. The remaining Athenians and Eretrians went back to their ships and swiftly retreated to Greece. The Greeks of Asia continued to fight with all available forces, buoyed by the fact that the Persians did not have a fleet in the region and could not deploy enough infantry to besiege any of the rebel cities. The revolt thus spread to other Persian domains around the Aegean. The Greeks sent military expeditions against cities located on the Hellespont and the Dardanelles that were under Persian political influence, in order to assume control over those strategic areas. They also persuaded Caria and Cyprus to revolt against the Achaemenids, obliging the Persians to use part of their forces against these rebelling provinces.

Caria was located on the coast in the south of western Anatolia. Being very near to Ionia and Aeolia, it had long been influenced by the Greeks. Cyprus had experienced a peculiar history after becoming independent from the Assyrians in 627 BC, the territory of the large island being divided into several small kingdoms that were heavily influenced by Greece but were later submitted by Egypt in 570 BC. Following the Persian conquest of Egypt, the Achaemenids also started to exert their influence over Cyprus. However, the Persians chose not to occupy the island with a large military force, instead permitted the local kingdoms to remain as semi-autonomous princedoms. Each Cypriot king acted as a local governor and each kingdom had to pay a yearly tribute to the Persians. Like the Greeks of Asia Minor before 499 BC, however, the Cypriots were just waiting for the right moment to launch a rebellion against the Achaemenids, an opportunity that came in 497 BC when they decided

Persian *takabara* infantryman armed with curved kopis sword.
(*Photo and copyright by Petar Chapkanov of Ancient Thrace*)

Persian *kardakes* infantryman equipped with crescent-shaped pelte shield and linen cuirass.
(*Colour plate by Patricio Greve Moller, copyright of Gabriele Esposito*)

to join the Greeks in their struggle. The Persians gathered a large fleet to retake the island, mostly thanks to the help of the Phoenicians (who were long-time commercial rivals of the Cypriots). The rebels of Cyprus asked for Greek help, and a fleet was sent to support them from Ionia. In the ensuing naval battle, the Greeks soundly defeated the Phoenician warships, yet they were not able to prevent the Persians from disembarking their soldiers on the island. The Cypriots clashed with the Persian expeditionary corps, but after a very harsh battle they were routed. At this point, with all hope of success gone, the Greek fleet sailed back to Asia Minor and the Persians were gradually able to reconquer the whole of Cyprus.

Meanwhile, the Achaemenids sent two smaller armies to the Hellespont and Dardanelles, where, one by one, all the cities freed by the Greek rebels were besieged and reconquered. The Carians, in the south, had assembled an army to face the Persians but were defeated during an initial clash. After this setback, they received reinforcements from Miletus and continued to resist. Another Carian defeat soon followed, but in 496 BC the Carians organized a very effective ambush against the main Persian military force fighting against them and thus temporarily gained the upper hand in the struggle. At this point, Aristagoras led an expedition into Thrace, probably with the intention of exploiting the great natural resources of that region (notably gold and silver) in order to support the revolt in Asia Minor. During this campaign, however, the great leader was killed, and all his projects of defiance against the Achaemenids thus came to nothing. By 494 BC, the Persians had mustered a large contingent of troops in central Anatolia and were ready to launch a final offensive against the Greeks of Asia Minor and Caria. A new Achaemenid fleet had also been assembled, whose presence was vital in supplying the land forces. The Persian army moved directly against Miletus and besieged it. Meanwhile the Greeks of Asia Minor decided not to fight on land against the invaders, and thus embarked their forces on all the warships that were available. The Greek fleet was assembled at the island of Lade, near the coast of Miletus, where it waited for the right moment to attack the Persian warships. In total, the Greeks had 353 triremes, a huge fleet for the standards of the time. Despite this, when the naval clash finally took place, it turned into a disaster for the Greeks, who were decisively defeated, many of their warships changing sides during the battle. Thereafter, Miletus was stormed and destroyed by the Persians. In the south of western Anatolia, some Carian strongholds continued to resist for a time, but by 493 BC the great Ionian Revolt was practically over. The Persians even occupied the islands of Chios, Lesbos and Tenedos, that had played an important part in the last phase of the rebellion, and were now very near to the borders of mainland Greece. The Persian retaliation against the rebellious Greek cities of Asia Minor was terrible, but did not last for long: the Achaemenids did not want to damage any further the economic capabilities of such a rich region of their empire. Instead of restoring the old tyrants to power, they accepted the new democratic forms of government and even started to respect the traditional Greek way of life without trying to modify it.

In 492 BC, the Persians organized a European expedition directed against Thrace, its main objective being the subjugation of the various tribes that inhabited the region. This operation was probably intended as a precursor of future offensives against Greece, the Persian army requiring a base on the European continent. The Persian expeditionary corps of 492 BC was led by Mardonius, son-in-law of Darius I, and departed from the Anatolian region of Cilicia (a strategically important territory linking southern Anatolia with Syria and the heart of the Persian Empire). The Persian army advanced overland to the Hellespont in northern Anatolia, marching along the coastline in order to retain direct contact with the fleet. All the troops were then embarked on the ships and crossed the Hellespont without particular problems. Once in Europe, the Persians focused on re-subjugating the Thracian tribes one by one. As these tribes were

Persian *kardakes* infantryman equipped with round Greek-style shield and thrusting spear. (*Colour plate by Patricio Greve Moller, copyright of Gabriele Esposito*)

Median light infantryman armed with spear, *akinakes* dagger and bow. (*Colour plate by Patricio Greve Moller, copyright of Gabriele Esposito*)

politically divided, the occupation of southern Thrace proved relatively easy for Mardonius. Having established a solid base in Europe, the Achaemenid army moved west to enter northern Greece. The Persians soon reached Macedonia, a semi-barbarous kingdom that at the time was of little political and military importance. The Macedonians were under a mix of influences, their 'Greek' character being no stronger than their Illyrian or Thracian one. During the European expedition of Darius I, the Macedonians had already recognized the Persians, albeit only formally, as their overlords; in 492 BC they did the same, and Macedonia thereby became a vassal state of the Persian Empire. Everything seemed to be working well for Mardonius, but at this point of the campaign he suffered an unexpected setback, the Persian fleet being hit by a terrible storm which destroyed most of its 300 ships. The Persian navy knew little of that part of the Aegean, meaning the disaster could well have been avoided. Whatever the case, the land forces were now left alone. Shortly after this event, the large Persian camp in Macedonia was attacked during the night by one of the most powerful Thracian tribes, the Brygians, who had not yet been fully subjugated. The surprise assault caused serious losses to the Achaemenids, with Mardonius among the many warriors wounded. At this point, with no support from the fleet, Mardonius decided to return to Asia Minor with all his forces, crossing back over the Hellespont using what remained of the fleet. Before withdrawing, however, the Persians crushed the Brygians and left some garrisons in Thrace and Macedonia. Although the European campaign of Mardonius ended in failure, it had secured for the Persians the land approaches to the Greek mainland.

In 491 BC, confident that the Greeks had been greatly impressed by the previous year's campaign in Thrace and Macedonia, Darius I decided that the time had come to annex mainland Greece to his immense empire. The Persians did not want to occupy the Greek cities with a large army, but simply to receive a formal submission from all the Greek *poleis*. The surrender ceremony required by the Achaemenids was a very symbolic one, including the offering of earth and water from the new subjects to the Great King. Persian ambassadors were sent to all the major Greek cities asking for this ceremonial offer of submission. But in Athens, the Achaemenid envoys were put on trial and then executed, while in Sparta they were simply thrown down a well. The Greek response to the Persian requests could not have been clearer. At this point, however, Sparta entered into a period of internal machinations due to a series of unexpected political events. The island of Aegina, unlike most of the other Greek communities, accepted Persian suzerainty. As a result, the Athenians feared that it could be transformed into a new naval base for the Persians, and thus asked the Spartans to intervene in order to deal with this problem. One of the two Spartan kings, Cleomenes, responded to the Athenian request for help and organized an expedition against Aegina. However, the other Spartan king, Demaratus, retracted his support to the military expedition and obliged Cleomenes to return. Cleomenes, having been humiliated under the eyes of the Athenians, declared Demaratus illegitimate and forced him to flee Sparta. Demaratus went into exile to the Persian court, where he became one of Darius's personal advisors, like the Athenian Hippias. Soon after these events, Cleomenes died unexpectedly, meaning Sparta had to replace both its kings in a very short time. Demaratus was replaced by his cousin Leotychides, while Leonidas took the place of Cleomenes. Meanwhile, the Athenians were able to submit Aegina, preventing the island from becoming an important naval base for the Persians.

After learning of the political instability that was afflicting Sparta, the Persians organized a military expedition against Greece for 490 BC. This was mostly intended as a punitive campaign of demonstration to show to all the Greek *poleis* that the Persian Empire was the most powerful state on earth. Athens and Eretria, the two cities that had directly supported the Ionian Revolt, were the main targets of the new Persian force sent to Europe. This army was assembled in the heart of the Achaemenid Empire at Susa and then marched to the coast of Cilicia in Anatolia. Here, the soldiers were embarked on the fleet that was waiting for them; this comprised 600 ships, some of them being warships and many others transport vessels (including for horses). The Persian army advancing against Greece in 490 BC was not particularly large, because Darius did not want to permanently occupy any of the *poleis*: he just wanted a demonstrative raid against Athens and Eretria, possibly destroying these two cities as an example to all the others. The ships thus transported about 25,000 warriors, including some 3,000 cavalry. With these numbers, the Persians could have easily defeated a single Greek city, but would have experienced serious difficulties in facing a Greek military coalition. As usual for the Achaemenid military practices of the time, the army comprised a core of Persian troops and some contingents of auxiliaries from various areas of the empire. The Persian fleet landed some troops on Naxos, which had repulsed an Achaemenid attack just before the outbreak of the Ionian Revolt. Most of the island's buildings were destroyed by the Persians, who enslaved many of the inhabitants. The fleet then moved against the island of Euboea to punish Eretria, with most of the army being landed to lay siege to the city. The Eretrians decided to remain inside the city walls rather than fight a pitched battle against a superior enemy. After six days of repulsed attacks against the city walls, the Persians were finally able to break into Eretria and razed it to the ground. All the surviving inhabitants were enslaved and the original city practically ceased to exist.

At this point, the Achaemenid fleet headed south down the coast of Attica, halting at the Bay of Marathon, where all 25,000 soldiers disembarked. The plain of Marathon was chosen by the Persians because it was quite near to Athens (being just

Persian foot archer carrying a rectangular body shield made of wicker and war hammer.
(*Colour plate by Patricio Greve Moller, copyright of Gabriele Esposito*)

Persian foot archer. Note the practice of transporting both the bow and arrows inside the leather quiver. (*Colour plate by Patricio Greve Moller, copyright of Gabriele Esposito*)

25 miles north of the city) and large enough to act as a base for their army. Indeed, soon after disembarking, a camp was built. With the Persian army at Marathon as an advisor was Hippias, the former tyrant of Athens, whom the Achaemenids intended to restore as the supreme leader of the Athenians after punishing the city. It was Hippias, according to some sources, who suggested the Bay of Marathon as a perfect landing place, the Persians having little knowledge of the territory. The Athenians soon assembled their army to face the invaders, sending 9,000 hoplites against the Persians. Only 1,000 heavy infantrymen remained in Athens to act as the city's garrison. The Athenians received no support from the nearby *poleis*, except for 1,000 hoplites sent by the small Boeotian city of Plataea. In order to emerge from the Theban sphere of influence, Plataea had formed a strong military alliance with Athens some years before. The Athenians had already defended Plataea from a Theban invasion, and thus the little city now felt it had to support Athens against the foreign menace. The Greek army marched to Marathon and blocked the two exits from the plain. But the Athenians were too few to confront the Persians in battle, choosing to await the arrival of other allied contingents. Philippides, Athens's greatest runner, was sent to Sparta in order to obtain some military support. He arrived in Sparta while the important religious festival of the Carneia was taking place, the Spartiates telling him that their army would move only after the end of the religious rites, ten days later. It is unclear whether the Spartans made this decision because of their religious zeal or because they wanted to see Athens destroyed by the Persians. Whatever the truth, the Athenians received no immediate help. After a stalemate lasting five days, knowing that no further reinforcements were on the way, the Athenians finally decided to attack before the Persians could move.

The Greek hoplites advanced in perfect close order towards the enemy, marching at their usual slow pace. In the centre of their formation they were arranged in a depth of four ranks, while on the two wings they were eight ranks deep. The Athenians thus wished to make a double envelopment of the enemy centre: the Persians would advance against the Greek centre, but would be heavily attacked from the flanks and the rear. When 200 metres from the enemy, before the Persian missiles could become effective against their ranks, the hoplites started to run and launched a devastating charge against the enemy infantry. The Achaemenid soldiers were taken completely by surprise, having never experienced close combat against an enemy bearing heavy equipment. Persian battles were usually fought from distance, using missiles against opponents who wore little or no armour. The Persian projectiles proved to be of no use against the armour and shields of the Greek hoplites. The Athenian wings quickly routed both the Persian flanks, where the auxiliary contingents were deployed. In the centre, the Persians were able to hold the line for some time but were eventually

Persian foot archer firing with his short bow.
(*Photo and copyright by Petar Chapkanov of Ancient Thrace*)

Persian slinger equipped with a small round shield and *akinakes* dagger. (*Colour plate by Patricio Greve Moller, copyright of Gabriele Esposito*)

encircled and crushed like the rest of the army. The defeated Persians fled in panic towards their ships, with the Greek hoplites in close pursuit. The disorganized Achaemenid retreat soon turned into a rout, and the Athenians were even able to capture seven enemy ships before the Persian fleet could escape from the Bay of Marathon. The battle was over and Athens had been saved from destruction: the Greeks had lost just 200 men, while around 7,000 Persians lay dead on the battlefield. The ancient world had never seen such a demonstration of military superiority, but the game was not yet over. The Battle of Marathon was just a small defeat in a far-flung corner of their empire for the Persians, but the Achaemenids could not tolerate the fact that a single Greek city had been able to rout their military forces. Consequently, they soon started to plan a further invasion of Greece, but this time with an overwhelming number of troops. The Spartans arrived on the battlefield of Marathon soon after the Persian defeat and were surprised by the manner of the Athenian victory: for the first time, they recognized the Athenians as fierce warriors. Athens had shown the Greek world that not only the Spartans could fight with such courage.

The balance of power was changing in Greece, but for the moment the Greeks had to prepare themselves for the obvious return of the Persians. The years 490–480 BC were characterized by a series of important events, which set the stage for the Second Greco-Persian War. Soon after Marathon, Darius I started to form a new army for a second and more devastating attack against Greece. In 486 BC, however, Egypt rose up in revolt and the Achaemenids had to use this new army in their African province. The Egyptian revolt proved very difficult to put down, forcing an indefinite postponement of the new expedition against the Greek *poleis*. In 486 BC, Darius died and the Persian throne passed to his son, Xerxes I, who also inherited the difficult task of reconquering Egypt. After this was finally achieved, the Achaemenids resumed their preparations for the invasion of Greece: materials and provisions of every kind were stockpiled in great quantities, while many thousands of warriors were recruited from every province of the Persian Empire. Xerxes decided that his immense army would cross the Hellespont in order to reach Greece, instead of landing on the coast, as his father had ordered in 490 BC. To do this, the Persians built two new bridges of boats across the Hellespont that were much larger and more solid than that erected for Darius's European campaign. The soldiers who made up the massive army of Xerxes came from forty-six different ethnic groups, each equipped according to their military traditions. During the autumn of 481 BC, the army was mustered in Anatolia, where it underwent final preparations. The number of soldiers who made up the Persian army has long been disputed, because Greek contemporary sources all give incredibly high numbers. Considering the manpower available to Xerxes and the strategic situation of all the areas of his empire, it is reasonable to conclude that the Persian army invading Greece in 480 BC probably numbered some 200,000 men. This was still an impressive number for the standards of the time, especially considering the military resources of Greece. During the subsequent operations, the Achaemenid land forces were to be supported by their fleet, as the army was to march along the coastline and receive constant supply and reinforcements from the ships. The Persian navy deployed a total of some 1,200 vessels (both warships and transport vessels) for the expedition.

In the years following the Battle of Marathon, Athens witnessed the rise of Themistocles, a very popular political leader who had the support of the lower social classes. Themistocles considered the Battle of Marathon as the perfect starting point from which to build an Athenian naval empire to control the whole eastern Mediterranean. Upon assuming power democratically, he started to use all the economic resources of his city to enlarge the Athenian fleet. With hundreds of triremes, the Athenians would be able to repulse any Persian attack against Greece and effectively defend all their new commercial routes. The Athenian merchants dominated all the markets of the Aegean, while the Athenian admirals exerted a strong political influence over all the coastal regions and islands of Greece. This naval programme launched by Themistocles was made possible by the unexpected discovery of a new seam of silver in the Athenian mines of Laurium. The newly excavated silver was used to finance the construction of hundreds of new triremes. By 480 BC, Athens could deploy the best and largest fleet in Greece, made up of modern vessels constructed using the most recent methods. The naval programme of Themistocles also had an important social consequence, since it permitted the permanent employment of thousands of poor citizens as rowers for the fleet. In 481 BC, when it became clear that the Persians were preparing another invasion of Greece, a congress of *poleis* was organized in Corinth to create a defensive military alliance against the Achaemenids. Athens and Sparta played a prominent role in this meeting, temporarily at least putting aside their increasing rivalry. Of the over 700 Greek states that existed at the time, however, only seventy sent representatives to the assembly at Corinth and joined the new alliance. Among the most important absentees were Argos and Thebes. Argos, an enemy of Sparta, decided to remain neutral in order to await the anticipated defeat of their rivals. Thebes, meanwhile, an enemy of Athens, was ready to support the Persians if this would help the consolidation of Theban hegemony over Boeotia.

In April 480 BC, the Persian army, with Xerxes in command, crossed the Hellespont and entered Thrace. The Achaemenids had already stored large amounts of food here during the years that preceded the invasion and had augmented these with the

Persian cavalryman wearing a corselet made of leather and bronze. He is armed with two throwing spears. (*Colour plate by Patricio Greve Moller, copyright of Gabriele Esposito*)

Persian cavalryman wearing a corselet of padded armour. His sword is of the kopis type.
(*Colour plate by Patricio Greve Moller, copyright of Gabriele Esposito*)

help of the Thracian communities. Upon hearing of the Persian moves, there was another meeting of the Greek alliance, during which the Thessalians proposed to assemble an army and stop the invaders at the northern borders of Thessaly: this was the only extensive flat region in Greece, where excellent war horses could be found and the local rulers could supply large numbers of cavalry. If conquered by Xerxes, Thessaly would become the perfect base for the Achaemenids in Greece, with the numerous horses of his army having access to plentiful pasture to even survive a winter. The Greek assembly accepted the Thessalian plan and sent an army of 10,000 hoplites to northern Thessaly. The Greeks did not have a precise idea of their enemy's numbers, but hoped to stop the Persians by defending a narrow mountain pass. Meanwhile, Xerxes entered Macedonia, where Alexander I ruled as a vassal of the Great King. The Macedonians put up no resistance, but passed on some crucial information to the Greeks: that their proposed defensive positions could be bypassed by at least two other mountain passes, and that the Persian army was much bigger than anticipated. Hearing this, the Greek army retreated, abandoning Thessaly. Consequently, the Thessalians joined the Persian host and did not oppose the Achaemenid advance across their lands. At this point, the Greeks decided to halt their retreat and to make a stand, selecting another narrow mountain pass located north of Attica and Athens, where a small army of hoplites could try to stop Xerxes. The chosen place, known as the Pass of Thermopylae, held the key to access to central and southern Greece, where Athens, Thebes, Argos, Corinth and Sparta were all located. Despite Thermopylae being so important strategically, not all the Greeks considered its defence as of primary importance. The Peloponnesian cities, including Sparta, preferred to organize a line of defence at the Isthmus of Corinth in order to protect their cities, but this would have resulted in the destruction of Athens and Attica. In the end, however, the strategic line supported by Leonidas of Sparta and Themistocles of Athens prevailed: the Greeks would send an army to Thermopylae, supported by their fleet, the narrow pass being located close to the coast.

Leonidas faced strong opposition in his city because the Persian attack happened while the important religious festival of the Carneia was taking place (just like ten years before, when the Persians came ashore at Marathon). The Spartans could not move due to religious restrictions, and thus could not send their army to Thermopylae. Nevertheless, Leonidas, had no intention of cause the destruction of Greece for such a futile reason, defying convention by marching with just the 300 hoplites of his royal bodyguard to the pass. These men, the best of all the Spartan warriors, answered not to the Spartan state but only to the king, who could deploy them as he pleased, on every occasion and in every place. Like most of the elite Greek troops of the time, these 300 soldiers were probably mounted infantrymen,

Babylonian heavy infantryman equipped as a spearman with scale cuirass. (*Colour plate by Patricio Greve Moller, copyright of Gabriele Esposito*)

Assyrian heavy infantryman equipped with pointed helmet and round shield. (*Colour plate by Patricio Greve Moller, copyright of Gabriele Esposito*)

moving on horseback to travel long distances very quickly, but dismounting to fight as normal hoplites once the battlefield was reached. Known as *Hippeis*, they were all veterans. Indeed, before departing from Sparta, Leonidas had ordered that all the younger members of his bodyguard be replaced with experienced Spartans who already had sons. Thus, the blood lines of the best Spartan warriors would not be lost if all the *Hippeis* were killed in battle. The 300 chosen soldiers were accompanied by 900 servants, known as Helots, with three for each hoplite. As a result, the Spartan force numbered 1,200 soldiers: 300 heavily armed hoplites and 900 Helots equipped as auxiliary light infantry. The small Spartan contingent was reinforced en route by troops sent from various *poleis* of the Peloponnese, which had strong political links with Sparta. In total, less than 3,000 others joined the Spartans, made up of the following contingents: 500 Mantineans, 500 Tegeans, 1,200 Arcadians, 400 Corinthians and 200 Phelioans. With these 4,000 fighters, Leonidas reached the Pass of Thermopylae and established a strong defensive position. He soon received a further 3,000 reinforcements from other Greek cities that had originally agreed to help stop the Persians at the pass: 700 Thespians, 400 Thebans, 1,000 Phocians and 1,000 Locrians. Leonidas's army now mustered some 7,000 soldiers, who were about to face the entire Persian army of Xerxes.

Upon reaching Thermopylae, the Spartan king decided to camp at and defend the narrowest part of the pass. Known as the 'middle gate', this had already been fortified by the Phocians with the construction of a defensive wall. Before the Persians' arrival, Leonidas had his men enlarge and reinforce the existing wall. The Spartans were informed by locals that the pass could be outflanked by a little-known mountain track, which had not been used for many years. Fearing that the Persians could find it, Leonidas sent the 1,000 Phocians to garrison the mountain path and guard the rear of his army. When the Persian army arrived at the pass, Xerxes immediately saw that the Greek position was a very strong one that would be difficult to overcome. His immense army would have to fight in a very narrow space, being unable to deploy its great numerical superiority. The Great King sent an ambassador to Leonidas with peace proposals, but these were refused by the Greeks. The Persians then waited for four days before attacking, in the hope that the allies of the Spartans would abandon Leonidas after seeing the vast size of the Persian army. However, all the Greek contingents maintained their positions, ready for the Persians to launch their assault. To begin the battle, Xerxes ordered his 5,000 archers to open fire on the Greeks from distance, but their missiles caused no damage to the hoplites, who were heavily protected by their shields. At this point, the Achaemenid monarch ordered a series of frontal assaults, with waves of 10,000 men attacking. These were all repulsed by the Greeks, as the Persians had no experience of close combat and had very little space for manoeuvre inside the confines of the pass. The Greeks rotated their contingents of hoplites in the front line, meaning they always had fresh soldiers facing the attackers. Furthermore, the spears of the Persian infantrymen were too short to engage the hoplites and the numerical superiority of the attackers was of no use in such a narrow pass. Before the first day of battle was over, Xerxes launched a final assault with the 10,000 chosen warriors of his royal guard: these were the famous Immortals, experienced warriors considered to be the best infantry of the Persian army. However, the Immortals were also repulsed, suffering very high losses.

On the second day of the battle, the Persians continued their frontal infantry assaults, but again they were thwarted on each occasion. Xerxes was then informed of the existence of the mountain path around the pass. During the following night, the Immortals were guided along this track behind the Greek army, thereby encircling their opponents. At daybreak of the third day, the Immortals attacked the Phocians who were guarding the rear of the Greek army. The Phocians retreated to a nearby hill and tried to resist, but could not stop the Persian advance. At this point in the battle, it became clear to the Greeks that they had been encircled and there was no hope of victory. Leonidas, as commander-in-chief, gave his allies the option to retreat with honour while he remained to defend the pass with his Spartans. Eventually, most of the Greeks abandoned Leonidas, but the Thespians and the Thebans remained, as well as the Helots, who as servants of the Spartans had no say in the matter. By the time the Battle of Thermopylae took place, the city of Thebes had already joined the Persians, as had Macedonia and Thessaly. The exact nature of the Theban hoplites who fought with Leonidas at the pass is thus unclear. According to the few sources available, these Thebans were not sent to fight against the Persians by their *polis*, but were volunteers who decided to support the Greek cause and abandon their own city. It is known for sure that many citizens in Thebes were opposed to the decision to forming an alliance with the Achaemenids. This would explain why they refused to abandon the field of battle when defeat became clear for the Greeks. Leonidas's last stand had not only symbolic implications, but also some practical ones: thanks to his prolonged resistance, more than 3,000 Greek allies were able to escape from the trap and live to fight again for the freedom of Greece. The last phase of the battle was terrible for both sides. Most of the hoplites were now fighting with their swords, the majority of the spears having been broken in earlier combat. Despite the Persians' massive numerical superiority, they still suffered terrible casualties. Some 10,000 Persians attacked the Spartans and their remaining allies from the front and another 20,000 (including the Immortals) advanced from the rear. In the end, all the Greeks, including Leonidas, were killed after retreating to a small hill. Considering that 3,000 Greeks escaped from the battlefield before the final assault, and that most of the

Phocians in the rearguard were able to survive, Greek casualties amounted to around 3,000 men (including all the 1,200 Spartans). The Persian army suffered some 20,000 casualties in just three days of battle for a narrow pass – 10 per cent of their total forces. The route to the heart of Greece now lay open for the invaders, but the Greeks still had important military resources to use in the struggle: the main Spartan army and the Athenian navy were still intact.

While these dramatic events took place on land, the combined fleet of the Greek *poleis* clashed with the Persians warships at Cape Artemision. Themistocles supported the land forces deployed at the Pass of Thermopylae by guarding their exposed flank on the coast. To do so, he assembled the vessels under his command at Cape Artemision, a very important strategic maritime position, comparable to that of Thermopylae on land. The cape was not far from the narrow mountain pass, on the northern tip of Euboea, dominating the only entrance to the small channel that divided Euboea from mainland Greece and thus from Thermopylae. If the Persians entered this channel, Leonidas could have been attacked from his seaward flank and the Persian navy could have landed troops in Attica. Themistocles's fleet included about 270 triremes: 127 were sent by Athens, forty by Corinth and the others by several different city states, including ten from Sparta. The Greeks maintained their positions at Cape Artemision for three days, just like troops at the Pass of

Babylonian medium infantryman armed with spear and bow. (*Colour plate by Patricio Greve Moller, copyright of Gabriele Esposito*)

Assyrian archer wearing heavy personal equipment that comprises pointed helmet and scale cuirass. (*Colour plate by Patricio Greve Moller, copyright of Gabriele Esposito*)

Thermopylae, the two battles taking place at the same time. During the first day of the naval clash, the Greeks repulsed an enemy assault and launched a highly effective counter-attack. The waters of Cape Artemision were too narrow for the immense Persian fleet, which could not manoeuvre effectively. The following day, both sides reorganized their forces and nothing of note occurred. On the third and final day of the naval battle, both sides fought courageously and suffered extremely high losses before retiring to their starting positions at nightfall. The Greeks had resisted for another day, but by now it was clear that they had to change strategy, Themistocles having been informed that Leonidas had been killed and that the position at Thermopylae had fallen to the Persians. The Greek naval commander had no choice but to evacuate Cape Artemision as soon as possible in order to defend Attica and the rest of Greece. The Greek fleet retreated to the island of Salamis, off the western coast of Attica and not far from the port of Athens (Piraeus). Since the Athenian army was embarked on the fleet and the Thebans had joined the Persians, there were no more Greek troops located north of the Isthmus of Corinth that could defend Attica. As a result, the population of Athens was taken on board by the fleet and transported to the island of Salamis. Meanwhile, Sparta and all the Peloponnesian cities (with the exception of Argos) started to prepare a strong defensive line on the Isthmus of Corinth, building a wall and demolishing roads.

During the following days, Athens was occupied by the Persian army and completely destroyed: very little of the city remained, but most of the Athenians were still alive and safe on the island of Salamis. Themistocles remained in his position at Salamis and awaited the arrival of the Persian navy, planning to fight another naval battle against the Achaemenids in the narrow Straits of Salamis, where the great agility of the small Greek vessels would cause serious problems to the larger, less manoeuvrable warships of Xerxes. Against all odds, events went exactly as planned by Themistocles. The Battle of Salamis ended in disaster for the Persians, who lost more than 200 warships and with that their naval superiority. At this point of the war, the strategic situation of the two sides changed considerably: the Greek naval forces were now free to move across the Aegean and could have easily destroyed the bridges built by the Persians to cross the Hellespont. This would isolate the Persian troops in Europe, with no possibility of retreat to Asia or to receive reinforcements. The Persian army in Greece was still very large and strong, but without the support of the fleet it would experience serious difficulties in seizing the enemy defences on the Isthmus of Corinth. If 7,000 hoplites had defended the Pass of Thermopylae for three days, the combined Spartan and Peloponnesian armies would have been able to thwart the Persians at the Isthmus for many months. Understanding this dramatic change in the strategic situation, Xerxes decided to leave Greece with a substantial part of his army

Assyrian cavalryman armed with spear and bow as well as with sword. (*Colour plate by Patricio Greve Moller, copyright of Gabriele Esposito*)

and to cross the Hellespont before the Greeks could attack the bridges there. He left behind a force of some 80,000 chosen warriors (mostly Persians and Scythians) under the command of Mardonius. The earlier numerical superiority of the Persians had now vanished, meaning the Greeks could launch a counter-offensive to expel the foreign invaders from their lands.

Mardonius retreated to Thessaly to reorganize his forces during the winter of 480–479 BC. Meanwhile, the remnants of the shattered Persian fleet went to Samos, having no intention of facing Themistocles again in battle. During the spring of 479 BC, after months of preparations, the Persians moved south again and advanced towards Athens, reoccupying the empty ruins of the city. This time, however, the Greeks assembled all their land forces to create a large single to fight a decisive pitched battle. The Spartan-led army crossed the Isthmus of Corinth and marched north out of the Peloponnese to free Attica. Learning of this, Mardonius retreated back to Boeotia, where he could count on the military support of Thebes and the flat terrain was perfect to employ the large contingents of Persian cavalry. Mardonius ordered the construction of a fortified camp at Plataea, north of the Esopus River in Boeotia. He waited there for the arrival of the Greek army

Phoenician naval officer equipped with a linothorax cuirass reinforced with bronze scales. (*Photo and copyright by Denis Taverne of Make Carthage Great Again*)

with his 80,000 Persians and 20,000 soldiers sent by Thebes and other Greek allies (Boeotians, Thessalians and Macedonians). The Greek army, commanded by the new Spartan regent, Pausanias, comprised some 40,000 hoplites: 10,000 Spartans, 8,000 Athenians, 5,000 Corinthians and 27,000 soldiers from several minor city states.

When the Greeks arrived at Plataea, Mardonius launched a series of minor cavalry raids against them in order to lure Pausanias down to the plain between the two armies, where the superior Persian cavalry could be employed more effectively. During one of these raids, Mardonius's cavalry was able to block the only source of water available to the Greek army, the Gargaphian Spring. Eight days later, the Greeks finally decided to retreat to a better position where fresh water was available. This difficult movement was conducted at night under the cover of darkness, but its only result was to fragment the Greek line of battle before sunrise. Mardonius, realizing that he now had an opportunity to crush the enemy, launched a general assault against the retreating Greeks, who were moving in complete disorder. Most of their contingents were isolated from each other, as they did not retreat at the same pace and did not follow the same route. The ensuing clash was a very confused battle, during which individual Greek formations were able to repulse and then defeat the attacking Persians. The Spartans bore the brunt of the fighting, causing terrible losses to the Achaemenids. The Athenians also fought extremely well, defeating the Theban hoplites after hours of violent close combat. In the last phase of the battle, the Greek army was able to break the Persian defences and destroy their camp, transforming Mardonius's retreat into a rout. The Persian army was practically destroyed, suffering some 80,000 casualties, including Mardonius himself. Greek losses were said to amount to just 1,500 men. Meanwhile, in the Aegean, the remnants of the Persian navy had abandoned Samos and retreated back to the Ionian coast of Asia Minor at Mycale. Here, the Persians beached their ships and built a defensive palisade around them: they had no intention to fight with the Greeks at sea again, merely wanting to preserve what remained of their fleet. The Greeks followed the Persians to Mycale and disembarked troops on the Ionian coast with the objective of destroying the new enemy base. The Greek force numbered 40,000, but only part of them were hoplites. Facing them were 60,000 Persians, many of them being sailors rather than soldiers. The Persian contingents from Asia Minor then changed sides and joined the other Greeks, helping them in the final part of the battle. A total of 40,000 Persians were killed and all the beached Achaemenid ships were destroyed, as well as the fortified camp of Mycale. The Persian navy had been eradicated, leaving the Greeks as masters of the Aegean and able to go back to Greece after checking with their own eyes that the Persians had destroyed the bridges across the Hellespont.

Phoenician naval infantryman wearing a full set of heavy equipment. The crested helmet, cuirass made of leather and sword with curved blade all show a certain Greek influence. The harpoon was a distinctive weapon of the Phoenician marines. (*Colour plate by Patricio Greve Moller, copyright of Gabriele Esposito*)

Phoenician naval infantryman wearing a corselet of scale armour. (*Photo and copyright by Denis Taverne of Make Carthage Great Again*)

The second Persian invasion of Greece had ended, but the war between the Greek world and the Persian Empire was not yet over. After Mycale, most of the Greeks wished to enter a new period of stability and peace. They had not desire to continue fighting against the Achaemenids now that the Persian menace was over. Among the Greeks, however, the Athenians had a different opinion. They were in the process of rebuilding their city, that had been destroyed by the Persians, and had no intention of renouncing to their political ambitions. They now had full control over the Aegean and could deploy the largest fleet in the Mediterranean world. After the terrible sacrifices of 490–478 BC, they wanted to capitalize on the current situation in order to build a naval empire that could fill the vacuum left by the Persians. As a result, they continued to launch offensive operations against the last Persian strongholds resisting in the Aegean. The Chersonese, a peninsula on the southern coast of Thrace, was still in Persian hands. The Achaemenids continued to garrison the area, from their base of Sestos, as it was the place where the two bridges crossing the Hellespont had been built and where new bridges could be constructed for future invasions of Europe. After a difficult siege that lasted several months, the Athenian navy was able to take Sestos, capturing all the materials that had been employed to build the bridges over the Hellespont. All the Persian garrisons of the Chersonese were captured or destroyed in the following weeks, with the help of some local Thracian tribes. The Greeks, who were still acting in accordance with the terms of the alliance formed in 480 BC, then decided to attack Cyprus. However, the Spartans decided to leave the Hellenic Alliance, and were soon followed by most of their Peloponnesian allies. It was by now clear that the original anti-Persian military alliance was transforming itself into a naval coalition led by Athens, with the main political objective of substituting Persian influence over the eastern Aegean with that of the Athenians. The Spartans, worried about the ascendancy of Athens, had no intention of helping any of their Greek allies to become even more powerful. After Sparta and other cities left the original alliance, the remaining members changed its name to the Delian League. The new alliance was under strong Athenian leadership, since no other Greek *polis* but Sparta could deploy the military resources available to Athens. From 478 BC, the Delian League continued to fight against the Persians in every corner of the eastern Mediterranean, mostly to expand the Athenian sphere of influence over Asia Minor. By forming the new military alliance, the Athenians offered a choice to all those cities that wished to become part of it: each member of the Delian League could contribute to its military operations by sending soldiers and ships or paying a tax to help finance the Athenian war effort. Most of the cities, tired of war, chose to pay the tax in exchange for Athenian military protection. Thanks to the victories of the Persian Wars, the Athenians had become a great regional power that rivalled Sparta, forming a major alliance to counter-balance that of the Peloponnesian League created long before by Sparta.

The first military action of the Delian League against the Persians was an attack on Cyprus in 478 BC. As we have seen, the island had long been heavily influenced by Greek culture and was inhabited by a large number of Greeks, many of whom were rich merchants or experienced artisans. As a result, together with Asia Minor, Cyprus was one of the Delian League's main targets. The Athenians were able to expel the Persian garrisons and restored the formal independence of the minor local kingdoms, who in return had to accept the suzerainty of the Delian League. As Cyprus was seen as a secondary dominion by the Persian Empire, the Achaemenids made no serious attempt to reconquer it during the following decades. The small kingdoms of the island, however, did not easily accept Athenian protection and revolted at least twice against the Delian League: in 460 BC and 451 BC. The second revolt of 451 BC was a major one, with the Athenians having to send a fleet of 140 warships in an attempt to quell it. However, unexpectedly, the Cypriot kingdoms were able to resist and wait for the arrival of a Persian fleet. The Achaemenids sent a large expeditionary corps, which joined forces with the rebels. The decisive battle of the campaign was fought at sea at a location off the coast of Cyprus known as Salamis, the same name as the earlier naval battle that had been fought in 479 BC. The Athenians were again able to prevail, soundly defeating the Persian fleet. Nevertheless, after the clash, the Greeks realized that Cyprus was lost unless they were willing to reconquer the island and garrison it with thousands of soldiers, something they could not afford to do at that moment due to their involvement on other fronts.

In the years following 478 BC, the Delian League protected the independence of the Greek cities in Asia Minor – which had been freed after Mycale – and extended its influence over the coast of Thrace and into the Black Sea. In 469 BC, the Persians assembled a large fleet at the mouth of the Eurymedon River in southern Anatolia, intending to use their warships to launch a major campaign against the Greek city states of Asia Minor. After ten years of minor defeats, the Achaemenids were slowly reorganizing themselves to face the Greeks again. The Delian League, however, became aware of the Persian movements and attacked first before fresh reinforcements could enlarge the enemy fleet at the Eurymedon River. The Persian fleet was taken by surprise, its warships being unable to reach the open sea. Most of them were destroyed on the sandbanks of the river and all the sailors fled before the Greeks could disembark. Near the fleet, the Persians had assembled a land army, whose camp the fleeing sailors entered. The Athenians then attacked the Persian camp and routed all those they encountered, in an exact repetition of the Battle of Mycale. After re-embarking on their ships, the Greeks moved to the open sea and

Phoenician naval infantryman equipped with a helmet made of bronze and a padded cuirass with leather plates on the shoulders. (*Colour plate by Patricio Greve Moller, copyright of Gabriele Esposito*)

defeated the naval reinforcements that the Persians had waiting off the Eurymedon River – numbering some eighty Phoenician warships – before sailing back to Greece. After such a severe defeat, the Persians were unable to send a fleet into the Mediterranean for more than a decade, until 451 BC, when they tried to help the revolt of Cyprus against the Delian League, as related above. All Achaemenid plans for the reconquest of Asia Minor had to be cancelled too. In 460 BC, after the series of pre-emptive strikes described above, the Athenians decided to adopt a much more offensive strategy in order to expel the Persians from most of the eastern Mediterranean. The Delian League's new objective was Egypt, one of the last regions conquered by the Achaemenids and a province of the Persian Empire that had revolted on several occasions against its overlords. The last major Egyptian revolt had taken place in 486 BC and had been crushed by the Achaemenids. The Athenians now wished to foment a new revolt, one which would be massively supported by their fleet. An independent Egypt, allied with the Delian League, was seen as a perfect outcome for the expansionist Athenians.

Phoenician naval infantryman equipped with linen cuirass and round shield. (*Photo and copyright by Denis Taverne of Make Carthage Great Again*)

In 461 BC a revolt, probably instigated by the Athenians, started in Egypt. This was led by a local ruler named Inaros, who came from the Libyan desert bordering western Egypt. Once most of the country came under the control of Inaros after the expulsion of the Persian garrison, he formally requested military help from the Delian League in view of the inevitable Achaemenid counter-offensive. The Athenians sent a powerful fleet of 200 warships to help the Egyptians. The expedition had three main objectives, which on paper appeared easy to gain: obtaining a naval base near the Nile Delta, getting full access to the massive grain production of Egypt and restoring the traditional trading links between Greece and Egypt. When the Greeks arrived, the Persians were still blocking the Nile Delta with a small force of fifty Phoenician warships. The Athenians attacked and destroyed this blockading fleet, sailing up river and then joining forces with the rebels. The Persians had already sent a large army to retake their Egyptian province, and this was stationed not far from the Nile Delta. Once the Athenians disembarked their troops, Inaros felt confident enough to lead his combined Greek and Egyptian army against the Persians. During the ensuing battle, the Achaemenid troops were routed, suffering terrible losses. The few survivors retreated back to the citadel of Memphis. The Greek-Egyptian army besieged the citadel of Memphis for four years without being able to take it. Finally, in 455 BC, a new Persian expeditionary corps of elite troops invaded Egypt and defeated the besieging force at Memphis. The Greeks then fell back to the island of Prosopitis in the Nile Delta, where their fleet was anchored. Here they were besieged by the Persians for 18 months, before the island was stormed and seized by the Achaemenids after digging some canals to reach Prosopitis from the mainland. The Athenians suffered very high casualties, only a few survivors being able to escape. The Egyptian revolt came to an end and a new Athenian squadron, arriving to reinforce Prosopitis when the island had already fallen, was also destroyed by the Persians, who attacked it from land and sea. After the disaster of this Egyptian expedition, the Delian League decided to make peace with the Achaemenids. In 448 BC, with the Peace of Callias, the lengthy hostilities between the Greeks and Persians finally came to an end after almost fifty years of war (494–448 BC). The peace treaty was centred around four fundamental points: all the Greek cities of Asia Minor were to remain part of the Persian Empire but would enjoy a large degree of autonomy and be able to live by their own laws; Persian armies could not enter the western part of Anatolia, located west of the Halys River; Persian fleets could not sail along the western coast of Anatolia, with Phaselis and the Cynaean Rocks being the last points they could reach respectively in southern and northern Anatolia; and the Delian League was to cease any military operations directed against the Achaemenid dominions in the Aegean and eastern Mediterranean (notably Cyprus and Egypt).

Phoenician naval infantryman wearing bronze helmet and leather cuirass. (*Photo and copyright by Denis Taverne of Make Carthage Great Again*)

Phoenician naval infantryman equipped with bronze helmet and round shield. (*Photo and copyright by Denis Taverne of Make Carthage Great Again*)

Chapter 4

The Consolidation of the Persian Empire

Artaxerxes I, who succeeded his father Xerxes I in 465 BC and ruled until 424 BC, was the Persian monarch who signed the Peace of Callias with the Greeks. Despite experiencing numerous difficulties, he was able to preserve the unity of the Achaemenid Empire and keep Egypt among the Persian domains. Artaxerxes was succeeded by his son, Xerxes II, but his reign was quickly characterized by political chaos, with two illegitimate sons of Artaxerxes questioning his ascendancy to the throne and revolting against their half-brother. The two pretenders to the throne, Sogdianus and Darius II, could count on the support of several satraps and thus controlled large portions of the Achaemenid Empire. Sogdianus ruled over Elam, while Darius II was supported by Media and Babylonia as well as by Egypt. Just a few weeks after his coronation, Xerxes II was assassinated in a plot organized by Sogdianus, who thereby secured control of the core of Persian lands, but he too was killed a few months later. Consequently, by the beginning of 423 BC, Darius II remained as the sole ruler of the Achaemenid Empire. The new king, despite being quite weak politically, carried out a strong anti-Greek foreign policy. He formed an anti-Athenian alliance with Sparta – which at the time was embroiled in the long and bloody Peloponnesian War with its great rival Athens – and reasserted Achaemenid control over several Greek cities of Asia Minor during 412 BC. Darius II died in 404 BC and was succeeded by his son, Artaxerxes II, whose reign was troubled from the outset by the rivalry existing between him and his younger brother, Cyrus the Younger. Cyrus started planning a major revolt soon after the ascendancy of his brother, counting on the military support of the satrap of Lydia as well as the Greek colonies of Asia Minor. Cyrus, differently from his older brother, favoured adopting a more conciliatory foreign policy towards the Greeks and was thus able to raise substantial numbers of professional mercenary soldiers in Greece. Initially, Artaxerxes II tried to avoid the outbreak of a full-scale civil war, opening negotiations with his brother. Yet these came to nothing after Cyrus established a formal alliance with Sparta and recruited a large contingent of Greek mercenaries. These consisted of 10,400 hoplites and 2,500 light infantry commanded by the Spartan general Clearchus. They became known to history as the 'Ten Thousand',

Jewish light infantryman equipped with throwing spears and round shield.
(*Colour plate by Patricio Greve Moller, copyright of Gabriele Esposito*)

Jewish archer armed with a bow and short sword. He is wearing a simple helmet made of leather. (*Colour plate by Patricio Greve Moller, copyright of Gabriele Esposito*)

one of their members being the famous historian Xenophon, who later wrote a detailed chronicle of the Greek mercenaries' participation in the Persian civil war.

Cyrus the Younger, at the head of his foreign army, marched against Artaxerxes II, who had assembled a powerful force of some 40,000 men, most of the troops of the Persian army having remained loyal to the legitimate monarch. The opposing armies met in 401 BC on the plain of Cunaxa, on the banks of the Euphrates River. The Greek mercenaries, deployed on Cyrus's right flank, charged the left wing of their opponents, despite being outnumbered. Nevertheless, they broke through the ranks of Artaxerxes's men and started outflanking the king's army. On the other side of the battlefield, however, Cyrus was killed by a javelin while leading his cavalry against those commanded by his brother. This had a deep impact on the morale of Cyrus's troops, who began to flee from the battlefield in disorder. Only the Ten Thousand stood firm and kept their positions, under the guidance of Clearchus. Artaxerxes's men did not try to overcome the Greek mercenaries, who were heavily armoured and well-trained, making them more than a match for the Persian fighters. However, the camp of Clearchus's men was raided and the Greeks' food supplies were captured. Following Artaxerxes's victory at Cunaxa, the Ten Thousand found themselves far from home with no supplies and no employer. Being completely isolated in a territory that was controlled by their enemies, the Greek mercenaries had no choice but to march across a vast area of the Achaemenid Empire to reach the coast, from where they could set sail for Greece. Tissaphernes, one of Artaxerxes's leading satraps, set a trap for the Greek mercenaries by claiming to seek a compromise with them and inviting their commanders to a feast. Failing to recognize the treachery of Tissaphernes, all the senior Greek officers were taken prisoner and executed by the Persians, who hoped that this would convince the Ten Thousand to surrender. Instead, the mercenaries decided to continue their desperate march across the Achaemenid Empire, electing new officers to lead them, among them being Xenophon. The Greeks moved north to the Black Sea by crossing Armenia, being constantly harassed by the light troops of the Persian army, which followed them in close pursuit. The Persians, knowing they could not defeat a large force of well-armed hoplites on the open field, instead tried to destroy the Ten Thousand by waging a guerrilla war. The Greeks, suffering from a serious lack of food and water, were forced to march slowly in order to find the supplies they needed to survive. The Persians tried without success to block the movement of the Ten Thousand on several occasions. Xenophon proved himself an excellent military commander, avoided all the traps set by the Persians. Having fought many small-scale battles and suffered from every kind of hardship, the Greek mercenaries finally saw the Black Sea from the heights of Mount Theches. Here they shouted the famous cry '*Thalatta! Thalatta!*' ('The sea! The sea!'), as reported by

Arab light infantryman armed with throwing javelins.
(*Colour plate by Patricio Greve Moller, copyright of Gabriele Esposito*)

Armenian infantryman wearing a soft cap made of fur and armed with throwing javelins. (*Colour plate by Patricio Greve Moller, copyright of Gabriele Esposito*)

Xenophon in his *Anabasis* describing the plight of the Ten Thousand. After reaching the coastline, the mercenaries made contact with the local Greek colonies and started assembling a fleet that could transport them back to mainland Greece. However, it proved impossible for them to find the necessary number of ships, and the Ten Thousand were forced to change their plans. They moved south across Anatolia, with the forces of the satrap of Phrygia, Pharnabazus, in close pursuit. In 399 BC, after more battles and hardships, the Ten Thousand were finally able to cross the sea and disembark at Byzantium on the European coastline. They had endured one of the most incredible adventures in history and had managed to survive – despite having suffered severe losses – in the most hostile of conditions. The success of the Ten Thousand's lengthy retreat was mostly the result of Xenophon's skill, which later transformed the Athenian general into one of the greatest military commanders of Antiquity.

The reign of Artaxerxes II continued to be troubled even after the Ten Thousand left Asia. In 396 BC, the Spartan king, Agesilaus II, launched an invasion of Persian territories in Asia Minor. Artaxerxes, instead of facing the Spartans on the battlefield, used the vast financial resources of his empire to organize and fund a large anti-Spartan coalition in Greece. He sent enormous sums of money to the Greek cities of Athens, Thebes and Corinth in order to convince them to create a military alliance capable of destroying the political hegemony exerted by Sparta over most of Greece. Following their victory in the bloody Peloponnesian War, the Spartans had become the leading military power of the Hellenic world and started to nurture expansionist plans, including an invasion of the Persian satrapies in Asia Minor. Artaxerxes's diplomatic moves bore fruit, resulting in the outbreak of the Corinthian War during 395 BC. This saw the Athenians, Thebans and Corinthians all fighting against Sparta. Following the outbreak of this conflict, the Spartans were forced to suspend their invasion of Asia Minor in order to defend their homeland in mainland Greece. In 394 BC, the Athenian navy, with the support of the Persian fleet, destroyed Sparta's naval forces at the Battle of Cnidus, a major blow for Sparta which permitted the Athenians to raid the coastline of the Peloponnese. In 386 BC, having achieved his political objectives, Artaxerxes II betrayed his Greek allies and came to an arrangement with Sparta, signing the Treaty of Antalcidas. This led to the end of the Corinthian War and marked the beginning of the end for Sparta's supremacy over Greece.

Artaxerxes did not fight only against the Greeks during his reign, also having to face a major Egyptian revolt that erupted soon after his ascendancy to the throne. The Achaemenids tried to reconquer their Egyptian territories but without success, mainly due to the Egyptian rebels having allied themselves with Sparta. The Persians were forced to adopt a defensive approach for several years, and even had to repulse an

Egyptian invasion of Phoenicia. Following the end of the Corinthian War, however, Artaxerxes started preparing for a full-scale invasion of Egypt. In 377 BC, after 4 years of intense planning, Pharnabazus led an army of 200,000 soldiers – including 12,000 Greek mercenaries commanded by Iphicrates – against the Egyptian rebels. The Egyptians could deploy significant military forces, which included a sizeable number of Greek mercenaries commanded by the Athenian general, Chabrias. The Persians landed in Egypt near Mendes and advanced slowly towards Pelusium, hoping to face their enemies in a major pitched battle. However, this did not materialize, the Egyptians having flooded the areas crossed by the invaders and blocked navigable channels of the Nile with embankments. Despite this, the Achaemenids were able to penetrate into the Nile Delta and continue their advance for some time. However, the annual flood of the Nile then suddenly took place, halting all movement by the Persians. Several weeks passed without any success for the Persians, who were eventually forced to re-embark on their ships and return home. The failure of his Egyptian expedition was a major blow for Artaxerxes II, who had to face the Great Satraps' Revolt during the turbulent decade from 372–362 BC. Following the Egyptian campaign, many Persian satraps controlling the western provinces of the Achaemenid Empire rebelled against Artaxerxes II and tried to depose him. The revolt lasted for many years, being supported by Egypt as well as Sparta and Athens. In the end, however, the rebelling governors were all crushed by Artaxerxes, the eastern provinces of his empire having remained loyal to the king.

Artaxerxes II died in 358 BC and was succeeded by his son, Artaxerxes III, who inherited an Achaemenid Empire that was experiencing a series of problems. Soon after ascending to the throne, the new king tried to limit the secessionist ambitions of his western satraps by ordering them to disband the large numbers of Greek mercenaries that were under their orders. In 356 BC, however, the governor of Phrygia, Artabazus, revolted against Artaxerxes III and claimed the Achaemenid throne for himself. The rebellion was crushed by the monarch only after experiencing serious difficulties, ending in 353 BC when Artabazus fled to the Macedonian court as a political exile. The revolt had been supported by both Athens and Thebes, which worsened the diplomatic relations between the Persians and the Greeks. In 351 BC, Artaxerxes III tried to resolve one of the major problems inherited by his father, the secession of Egypt. He sent an army against the rebellious province – which had been acting as a fully independent state for several years – but his troops were unable to subjugate the Egyptians. The rebels could count on the decisive support provided by numerous Greek mercenaries, who were commanded by the Athenian general, Diophantus, and his Spartan colleague Lamius. Soon after the failure of the Egyptian expedition, Phoenicia and Cyprus also rebelled against Achaemenid rule. Artaxerxes III had

Greece under his rule. In September 338 BC, the court eunuch Bagoas, who had played a prominent role during the retaking of Egypt, orchestrated the poisoning of Artaxerxes III. Bagoas, intending to become the Persian kingmaker, assassinated several sons of the monarch before placing one of them – the young and weak Arses – on the throne.

Arses ruled for only a very short time, being poisoned by Bagoas when he tried to assert his independence. This turbulent period, characterized by court intrigues, significantly weakened the Achaemenid Empire, to the advantage of Philip II. The Macedonian king sent a military expedition with 10,000 men into Asia during 336 BC, having unified the whole of Greece under his control. Following the demise of Arses, Bagoas put Darius III on the throne of Persia. The new king was an aristocrat with a probable royal descent and a reputation for bravery. Darius, having obtained power, did not make the same mistake of his predecessor, having Bagoas killed as soon as possible. The new monarch, however, was soon obliged to deal with the Macedonians, who were invading his territories in Asia Minor. The Macedonian expeditionary force, despite being relatively small, occupied several coastal cities before the sudden assassination of Philip II halted it in its tracks. As we will see in the next chapter, the Macedonian invasion of the Achaemenid Empire resumed on a much larger scale under Philip II's son and successor, Alexander.

Chapter 5

The Fall of the Persian Empire

Alexander crossed the Hellespont at the head of his Macedonian troops in 334 BC. More than 100 triremes were needed to transport the Macedonian soldiers to Asia Minor, Alexander's army comprising some 37,000 men. The size of the army was impressive for the Greek standards of the time, with most of these soldiers being battle-hardened veterans with previous combat experience. However, if compared with the potential size of the Persian forces, which could oppose them, Alexander's military resources were puny. The Persian Empire has been heralded as the greatest state of the ancient world, having an immense territorial extent, stretching from Asia Minor in the west to India in the east, and from Central Asia in the north to Egypt in the south. To give an idea of the Persians' military resources, most of the individual satrapies were able to deploy an army with at least 30,000 warriors. Consequently, Alexander's Macedonian army only had the same numerical consistency as a single Persian provincial army – and Darius II had several such armies at his disposal. The Achaemenid armies comprised a myriad of different troop types, as all the peoples living within the Persian Empire had to contribute to the military efforts of the state by sending large contingents of warriors. These troops were equipped and fought according to the military traditions of their homelands. As a result, every kind of combat specialization could be found in the Persian army. It should be noted, however, that the Achaemenid armed forces had two structural weaknesses. Firstly, the army did not have a permanent nature like that of Macedonia, the Persian troops being mobilized only in case of necessity and thus not serving in times of peace. The only exception to this rule was the Immortals, the imperial guard of the Achaemenid rulers, who comprised a total of 10,000 chosen soldiers. The Immortals were always on active service and could be employed at any moment. The other Persian forces were only assembled into temporary divisions when needed. The second weak point of the Achaemenid military apparatus was the general lack of heavy infantry troops. Most of the peoples living inside the Persian Empire equipped their foot warriors as light skirmishers, armed with javelins or bows. Consequently, the Achaemenids had no heavy infantry contingents that could fight against the heavily armoured Greek hoplites (or phalangites) on equal terms. They tried to resolve this problem by recruiting increasing numbers of Hellenic mercenaries, but their loyalty

was always subordinate to the regularity of their payment. Bearing in mind the above, from a tactical point of view, each Macedonian phalangite corresponded to at least ten Persian skirmishers on the field of battle, meaning the great numerical superiority of the Achaemenids was matched by a massive qualitative superiority of Alexander's troops.

However, the Persians had a large and effective navy that was clearly superior to that of the Macedonians. They could have attacked Alexander's ships during their crossing of the Hellespont, but chose to avoid a direct confrontation. This proved to be the greatest strategic mistake made by the Achaemenids in their war against Alexander, but it should be borne in mind that the terrible memories of the Battle of Salamis were still fresh in Persia. Furthermore, Darius III, the supreme ruler of the Achaemenid Empire, did not consider Alexander and his comparatively small army of Macedonians a serious military threat. Indeed, he was convinced that the invaders would never be able to advance deeply into Asia Minor and had a very negative opinion of the Macedonian king. Memnon of Rhodes, the commander of the Greek mercenaries serving in the Persian army and one of Darius's main military advisors, suggested that rather than directly confronting the Macedonians, the Persians should adopt a prudent but effective scorched

Paphlagonian cavalryman wearing a crested helmet made of bronze. (*Colour plate by Patricio Greve Moller, copyright of Gabriele Esposito*)

Paphlagonian infantryman with headgear, closely resembling a Phrygian cap, made of leather. (*Colour plate by Patricio Greve Moller, copyright of Gabriele Esposito*)

earth strategy. By destroying all the food supplies in Asia Minor before Alexander could secure them, Memnon proposed, the Persians would cause a terrible logistical crisis for the Macedonian army that would oblige them to abandon their invasion. Memnon's strategic considerations were correct, since the invaders would have soon found themselves with a long supply line stretching across Anatolia. Once far from their bases on the coast of Asia Minor, the Macedonians would have been obliged to rely on the food resources of the areas that they were crossing and their supply lines would be dangerously exposed to attacks by Persian skirmishers.

Memnon's strategic advice, however, was promptly rejected by Darius and his generals. The Achaemenids felt they could not destroy the economy of their western satrapies just because a bold but inexperienced foreign king had landed in Asia. Instead, the Persians decided to mobilize the forces of their five Anatolian provinces and send them against Alexander as soon as possible to stop his advance. The clash between the Macedonians and the Anatolian satraps, known as Battle of the Granicus River, took place in May 334 BC, not far from the Hellespont. The army mobilized by the Persians for this first battle was not an extremely large, comprising just 40,000 men, meaning the Macedonians were not outnumbered. Between the opposing armies was the Granicus River, which the Persians attempted to use to their advantage. They did not attack the enemy, but instead waited for Alexander to move first. If they wanted to crush their opponents, the Macedonians would be obliged to cross the river under a hail of arrows from the Persians. This would have been an extremely dangerous manoeuvre, because the Achaemenids could have launched a sudden counter-attack while the Macedonians were crossing. Nevertheless, Alexander was undaunted, deploying his troops in a way that would become distinctive of his tactical vision: phalangites in the middle, heavy cavalry on the right wing and light cavalry on the left wing. The Macedonian king personally commanded his heavy Companion cavalry, who were tasked with launching the first attack against the Persian left. The clash began with a feint of the Macedonian left, which attacked the Persians in order to attract their attention. This move worked as planned, the Achaemenids sending significant reinforcements against the Macedonian light cavalry. Seeing that the Persian left wing had thus been weakened, Alexander launched the charge of his Companion cavalry. Deployed in their usual wedge formation, they crossed the Granicus without hesitation and smashed into the Persian centre, killing a great number of enemy infantry. The Achaemenids responded with a counter-attack using their best cavalry. During the ensuing melee between the mounted troops, the Macedonian king was wounded and risked being killed by a Persian who attacked him from the rear. However, one of Alexander's close friends, Cleitus, severed the outstretched arm of the Persian cavalryman who

Cilician infantryman equipped with a Phrygian helmet made of bronze, hoplite shield and deadly sickle sword.
(*Colour plate by Patricio Greve Moller, copyright of Gabriele Esposito*)

Lycian naval infantryman. The whole panoply shows a certain Greek influence despite being decorated in a quite peculiar way. The main weapon is a sort of pitchfork with two points. (*Colour plate by Patricio Greve Moller, copyright of Gabriele Esposito*)

was trying to kill Alexander, saving the life of his king. After some harsh fighting on the muddy banks of the Granicus, the mounted Companions prevailed over the Persian cavalry thanks to their long spears (the Achaemenid horsemen were armed only with javelins, which were of little use in close combat) and the support given to them by the elite hypaspist infantry. After opening a huge hole in the enemy formation, Alexander ordered a general advance of his phalanxes while attacking the Persian infantry with his heavy cavalry. His foot Companions could thus cross the Granicus unopposed and attack the Persian infantry from the rear. Alexander continued his advance, striking at the rear of the Persian cavalry that was fighting against his own light mounted troops. The attack of the phalangites sealed victory for Alexander, routing the Persian forces and obliging them to fall back in disorder. The Battle of the Granicus River was a great victory for the Macedonians with some 14,000 Persians killed or captured, against just 400 casualties for Alexander's men. The Persian army that fought at the Granicus River included a force of 18,000 elite Greek mercenaries commanded by Memnon of Rhodes, who acted as the overall Achaemenid commander during the battle. These were kept as a reserve, but were abandoned by the Persians when they fled. Surrounded by Alexander's cavalry, the Greek infantrymen were massacred: 10,000 of them were killed and the remaining 8,000 were captured by the Macedonians, who enslaved them and sent them back to Greece to work in Alexander's royal mines. Memnon, however, escaped. After destroying the army of the Anatolian satrapies, the Macedonians freed all the Greek cities of Asia Minor that had long been under Persian rule. Alexander was welcomed as a liberator by all the *poleis* of western Anatolia, who were granted the right of establishing forms of self-government based on democratic principles.

Against all expectations, the Macedonian king did not impose a strict rule over the lands that he had conquered. All the Persian satraps who surrendered to him without a fight were permitted to retain their administrative functions and the local populations could continue living according to their traditions. No attempts were made to impose Hellenic customs, and taxes were collected in a fair way. As a consequence, Alexander prevented the outbreak of revolts in his newly acquired lands by respecting the traditions and rights of the local people. After securing control of most of the Anatolian strongholds without fighting, the Macedonians moved to the very south of Asia Minor to besiege the only fortified city that was still in Persian hands: Halicarnassus. This was an important naval base of the Achaemenids and was garrisoned by a sizeable number of troops, under command of Memnon. After a brief but violent siege, the Macedonians opened a breech in the walls and stormed the city. Realizing that all hope of success had gone, Memnon abandoned his positions and ordered his retreating soldiers to burn Halicarnassus. Soon after these events, during

Carian infantryman equipped with a bronze crested helmet and round shield and armed with spear and drepanon reaping hook.
(*Colour plate by Patricio Greve Moller, copyright of Gabriele Esposito*)

Phrygian cavalryman wearing full heavy equipment. The crested helmet is highly decorated, the crescent-shaped shield shows a clear Thracian influence and the axe has a double blade. (*Colour plate by Patricio Greve Moller, copyright of Gabriele Esposito*)

a minor military operation, the Rhodian general was killed. After taking control of Halicarnassus, Alexander continued his march, crossing Cappadocia unopposed. He could now enter the rich Persian territories of Syria from the north, but to do this he had to cross the narrow mountain passes of the Taurus Mountains, commonly known as the Cilician Gates. These could have been easily defended by the local Achaemenid forces, but the Cappadocian satrap had no wish to fight Alexander. As a result, the Macedonians entered northern Syria unopposed.

While these events took place around the Taurus Mountains, Darius III finally started to recognize Alexander as a serious menace to the stability of his empire and began assembling a large army in the heart of his richest provinces. This time, the Macedonians would face the best soldiers of the Persian army, including the 10,000 Immortals. Darius advanced at the head of 100,000 soldiers against the invaders. The Persians did not attack the Macedonians directly, but manoeuvred from the east against their supply lines that stretched across the Taurus Mountains. Alexander was forced to march back to intercept Darius before he could cut the Macedonian supply lines running between southern Anatolia and northern Syria. This led to a battle being fought at Issus, on the coastline connecting Anatolia with Syria and near the mouth of the Pinarus River. The Macedonians were at a clear numerical disadvantage, but Alexander was not impressed by the superiority of his enemies. He deployed his forces in the usual way: light cavalry on the left (near the mouth of the Pinarus), phalanxes in the centre and heavy cavalry on the right. Darius concentrated all his cavalry on his right, near the mouth of the Pinarus. The Persians also deployed a substantial number of Greek mercenaries, some 12,000 in total, who were stationed in the centre of their line. The Achaemenids attacked first with their cavalry, which comprised a large number of heavily armoured horsemen, which invested the light cavalry of the Macedonian left that mostly consisted of Thessalians. Alexander responded by crossing the Pinarus at the head of his horse Companions and ordering a general advance of his infantry in the centre. This time the Macedonian infantrymen had some difficulties in crossing in front of the enemy, being opposed by Darius's Greek mercenaries. However, the hypaspists were soon able to punch a hole through the Persian left wing, at which point Alexander and his heavy cavalry launched a formidable charge against the Achaemenid centre and advanced against Darius. The Persian infantry was routed and suffered heavy losses, since its best elements (the Greek mercenaries) were already fighting against the phalangites and thus could not help Darius. Fearing for his life, Darius abandoned the battlefield before his army collapsed. Alexander then surrounded and attacked the Greek mercenaries, who were still resisting against the advance of the phalangites; these professional soldiers, like those of Memnon at the Granicus, did not surrender and thus suffered heavy losses. By the end of the battle, around 30,000 Persians had been killed, while the Macedonians suffered just 450 casualties. Alexander captured Darius's wife and daughters soon after the clash and was now free to occupy the rich regions of the Middle East.

The pride of the Persian army had been crushed and the reputation of Darius III as a military commander had been seriously damaged. After the Battle of Issus, the Achaemenid ruler tried to find a compromise with Alexander, having also lost part of his imperial treasure during the rout that followed the battle. Darius proposed a partition of Persian territories with Alexander: the Achaemenids would retain the eastern satrapies of the empire, while the Macedonians would exert control over those in the west. The Macedonian king rejected Darius's generous proposal and continued his advance across Syria. One of the richest regions of the Persian Empire, Syria was conquered very rapidly by Alexander. Moving south, the Macedonians occupied Phoenicia, corresponding to present-day Lebanon, which was of great strategic significance for the Achaemenids as it was where the Persian navy had its most important bases and arsenals. The coastal city of Tyre was the key military position in Phoenicia, the last major port of the Persians on the Mediterranean that had not yet been conquered by the Macedonians. Alexander understood that if his troops could occupy Tyre, the Persian navy would soon run out of supplies. Until that moment, both sides had avoided fighting a large naval battle, but for different reasons: the Macedonians did not have a very high opinion of the Greek sailors who made up the crews of their fleet, whereas the Achaemenids feared that the technological superiority of the enemy's warships could prove crucial in a clash at sea. As a consequence, both navies remained inactive during the early phase of Alexander's invasion. Over time, however, the Persians had lost all their ports, Alexander having followed a coastal path during his advance. He now had the opportunity to besiege Tyre and eliminate forever the menace represented by the Persian naval forces. The fortifications of the Phoenician city, however, were extremely strong, Tyre being enclosed by massive walls and connected to a nearby island that had two natural harbours on the landward side. After trying to find a compromise with the Tyrians by promising to respect their commercial interests, Alexander had no choice but to start the siege of the city in 332 BC.

Since the Macedonians could not attack Tyre from the sea, and the external walls of the city were too strong to be breached, Alexander ordered the construction of a 1-kilometre-long causeway that stretched out to the island located in front of Tyre. On paper, such an audacious project of military engineering seemed impossible, but the Macedonians were eventually able to build the causeway. It was used to move two massive siege towers (thought to be 150ft high) to the island. The Tyrians, fearing that

Phrygian peltast; the general appearance is pretty much that of a Thracian warrior. (*Courtesy of Association KORYVANTES/koryvantes.org; photo by Antonis Aliadis*)

Phrygian peltast equipped with crescent-shaped pelte shield.
(*Courtesy of Association KORYVANTES/koryvantes.org; photo by Antonis Aliadis*)

Alexander's plans could work, organized a counter-attack. Taking an old transport ship, they filled it with dried branches, pitch, sulphur and other combustible materials, then set the ship on fire and ran it up on the causeway built by the Macedonians. The counter-attack was a success, causing the destruction of the two siege towers.

Alexander now realized that he could never conquer Tyre without the support of his navy, which was still at the Hellespont transporting supplies. He therefore decided to assemble a new fleet by using the naval contingents provided to him by the recently conquered cities of Asia Minor. These consisted of eighty warships, the new fleet being augmented to 200 ships when the island of Cyprus sent another 120 vessels. Cyprus was still formally part of the Persian Empire, but the cities of the island had always enjoyed a high degree of autonomy. After the Battle of Issus, understanding that the Macedonians were on the verge of completing their conquest of Phoenicia, the various cities located on Cyprus (whose populations were mostly Greek) decided to support Alexander by sending him their fleets. With a naval squadron of 200 vessels, the Macedonian king could now blockade both ports of Tyre, preventing the arrival of supplies from the sea for the besieged Phoenicians. The Macedonians mounted battering rams on their warships and started to attack the fortifications of the island, trying to open a breach in the walls. When this duly happened, Alexander ordered a massive assault and bombardment. Although the defenders of Tyre put up a desperate resistance, in the end they were overwhelmed. Half of the city was destroyed and 30,000 of its inhabitants were captured to be sold as slaves.

With the conquest of Tyre, the Persian navy lost its last Mediterranean base and ceased to be a threat to the Macedonians. Alexander's next target was Egypt, one of the richest lands of the ancient world. Egypt had always been the most troublesome of the Achaemenid provinces. The Egyptians had never accepted Persian suzerainty, being proud of their glorious traditions. During the two centuries of Achaemenid rule, Egypt revolted against the Persians on several occasions and was able to regain independence for some brief periods. Alexander was thus sure that the Egyptians would join his cause with great enthusiasm and provide him with a large number of their excellent warships. Before entering Egypt, however, the Macedonians had to overcome the resistance of one final Persian stronghold that was located in the south of Palestine: the fortified city of Gaza. The siege of Gaza, which was built on a hill, proved an extremely difficult one, exactly like that of Tyre. The inhabitants of the city, together with their Nabatean allies, had no intention of surrendering, and indeed repulsed three assaults by the besiegers. The Macedonians suffered heavy casualties, and during one of their futile attacks Alexander himself was seriously wounded by an enemy arrow. When the Macedonian army was finally able to storm Gaza and crush the resistance of the defenders, all the male inhabitants of the city were killed, while women and children were sold into slavery. After the conquest of the last Persian stronghold in Palestine, Alexander could finally enter Egypt, where he was welcomed as a liberator by the local population and was made pharaoh. The Macedonians were surprised by the incredible enthusiasm of the Egyptians, who considered Alexander

Lydian heavy infantryman; the general appearance is that of a Greek hoplite, with bronze cuirass and round shield. (*Colour plate by Patricio Greve Moller, copyright of Gabriele Esposito*)

Lydian heavy infantryman equipped with Corinthian helmet, scale cuirass made of leather and pelte crescent-shaped shield. (*Courtesy of Association KORYVANTES/koryvantes.org; photo by Antonis Aliadis*)

the reincarnation of their gods Ra and Osiris. The Macedonian king showed great respect for Egyptian culture and religion. In addition, he left the administration of the country in the hands of the local ruling classes and initiated the building of a new coastal city that would be named Alexandria. Such acts did nothing but augment the love of the Egyptians for Alexander, who could now count on the country's massive amounts of grain and money.

In 331 BC, having completed the conquest of Egypt and the whole Mediterranean coastline of the Persian Empire, Alexander briefly reorganized his army in preparation for the most decisive of his battles. Until that time, the Macedonians had advanced along the coast in order to seize all the naval bases of the enemy fleet, a strategy that had worked well and meant Alexander could now exert total control over the eastern part of the Mediterranean. Now, however, the Macedonians had to move into the interior areas of the Achaemenid territories in order to face the bulk of Persia's military power. The Battle of Issus had been a brilliant victory for Alexander, but only 100,000 enemy soldiers had participated in it. The vast military resources of Darius III were still largely intact, meaning the pivotal clash of the war was yet to come. The theatre for this gigantic battle was Mesopotamia, probably the richest region in Antiquity where the first recorded civilizations of history had emerged several centuries before. Mesopotamia – the 'land between the two rivers' – was extremely fertile, being crossed by the Tigris and the Euphrates. These were the two most important waterways of the Middle East, and controlling their course was fundamental from a strategic point of view. Mesopotamia, together with present-day Iran, was the very heart of the Persian Empire. One of the empire's four capitals, Babylon, was located there, together with several other large cities. Darius knew that if he also lost Mesopotamia, it would have been impossible for him to save the Achaemenid Empire from collapse. As a result, he started to mobilize his full military potential for the pitched battle that would decide his destiny. Mesopotamia is a flat region entirely covered by vast plains, so the upcoming battle would be fought in conditions where the Persians could deploy their numerical superiority. When the Macedonians resumed their advance from Syria, Darius could have stopped them during the crossing of the Tigris or the Euphrates, which represented formidable natural barriers. Yet he did not attempt to attack Alexander while he was advancing, preferring to remain in the east in order to complete the mobilization of his forces.

The Persians had already fought two pitched battles with a river between them and their enemy, and both had ended in disaster. Now they wanted to restore their military reputation by defeating the Macedonian invaders on the open field. Darius was confident that sheer numbers would defeat Alexander and thus mobilized all the soldiers that were at his disposal, from every province of the Achaemenid Empire.

After crossing the Euphrates, the Macedonians followed a northern route instead of advancing on Babylon to the south-east. Alexander wanted to crush Darius before capturing the capital of Mesopotamia. After a short march, the Macedonians also crossed the Tigris in order to catch up with Darius, who was with his army on the eastern bank of the great river. The opposing armies came into contact at Gaugamela, present-day Tel Gomel, in the region of Kurdistan. When the Macedonians reached Gaugamela, their morale was very high – some days before, there had been a lunar eclipse that was interpreted as a positive omen for the destiny of Alexander. This time, however, Darius had chosen the battlefield well. Gaugamela consisted of a vast plain, the terrain having been flattened by the Persian soldiers before the arrival of the Macedonians. The Achaemenid monarch had assembled an immense army, with an estimated 150,000 warriors coming from every corner of the Persian Empire: 10,000 Immortals, 10,000 Greek mercenaries, 90,000 regular infantry and 40,000 cavalry.

In addition to these, Darius had three special shock troop types that he hoped would help decide the outcome of the battle in his favour: 2,000 heavily armoured cataphract cavalry from Bactria, 200 scythed chariots and fifteen Indian war elephants. The Persian plan was clear: they intended to launch a massive frontal charge on the flattened terrain with their three categories of shock troops in order to crush Alexander's phalanxes. The Macedonians had never previously faced scythed chariots or war elephants, so in Darius's view they would be unable to stop the Persian attack. The war chariots had scythe blades mounted on their wheels, which could hack men into pieces, while the war elephants were enormous beasts that again had never been seen before by the Macedonians. Scythed chariots had already been employed by the Persians on several occasions against different enemies and had always caused serious losses, being particularly effective against foot troops. Each chariot had two blades, about a metre long, mounted on its two wheels. It was pulled by a team of four horses and was manned by a crew of three men: one driver and two warriors. The main tactical task of the war chariots was to break through the lines of the enemy infantry, cutting down foot soldiers and opening huge gaps in their lines that could be exploited by the cavalry. During previous battles, the Persians had found that it was practically impossible to get horses to charge into the tight phalanxes of the Macedonians, which formed a wall of pikes when deployed in defensive formation. However, this problem could be solved by using war chariots to break the lines of the phalangites with their deadly blades. The tactical function of the war elephants was similar to that of the scythed chariots: to destroy everything they encountered, breaking the Macedonian pikes with their massive bodies (protected by armour) and trampling on the enemy foot soldiers. The 2,000 Persian cataphracts came from the border region of Bactria, in Central Asia, and were led by their ambitious governor, Bessus, an

Lydian heavy infantryman equipped with Illyrian helmet, scale cuirass made of leather and pelte crescent-shaped shield. (*Courtesy of Association KORYVANTES/koryvantes.org; photo by Antonis Aliadis*)

Scythian heavy cavalryman wearing a full set of scale armour. (*Photo and copyright by Scythian State*)

experienced military commander and the most powerful of the eastern satraps. The Bactrian cataphracts were fully armoured – with even their horses wearing massive scale-armour – and were armed with long and heavy spears that had to be used with both hands. Differently from the great majority of the Persian cavalry, the cataphracts were heavily enough equipped to face the Macedonian horse Companions on almost equal terms. In addition, they were trained to operate with the war chariots in order to charge across the gaps that the latter had opened up. To face Darius's mighty army, Alexander had some 47,000 Macedonian army warriors, comprising 31,000 heavy infantry, 9,000 light infantry and 7,000 cavalry. The Persians deployed their forces with the war chariots at the front, the infantry in the centre and the cavalry on the two wings. Shortly before the clash began, being overconfident about the capabilities of his charioteers, Darius decided to deploy the fifteen war elephants at the rear of his army as a strategic reserve to guard the Persian camp. The Macedonian line, having the same composition as their previous battles, was surpassed in length by the Persians by more than a mile, meaning it was inevitable that Alexander's army would be flanked by the Achaemenid troops. To guard against this, the Macedonian king deployed some of his heavy infantry behind his army in order to have a mobile reserve that could deal with any outflanking manoeuvre by the Persians.

The Battle of Gaugamela began with a general advance of the Macedonian phalanxes against the centre of the Persian army, to which Darius responded by sending most of his cavalry against the left wing of the enemy. Instead of supporting the phalanxes or sending reinforcements to his left wing, Alexander took command of his Companion cavalry and started to ride all the way to the edge of the Persian left wing that was located opposite him. This was mostly made up of heavy cavalry, comprising the Bactrian cataphracts under Bessus as well as some contingents of Scythians who were allies of Darius. Seeing that Alexander had prevented him from attempting a flanking manoeuvre in that part of the battlefield, Darius ordered Bessus and his elite cavalry to charge against the Macedonian king. A furious cavalry battle broke out between the two mounted contingents, during which the Macedonians came close to being defeated and Alexander himself was in great danger. The Bactrians and Scythians fought with enormous courage, and for the first time the horse Companions experienced serious difficulties against an enemy cavalry force. In the end, thanks to the arrival of some reinforcements consisting of the *prodromoi* light cavalry, Alexander prevailed against Bessus. The defeated Persians abandoned the battlefield and were closely pursued by the *prodromoi*, suffering large numbers of casualties. Seeing that his left wing had been destroyed and that the phalanxes were set to smash his centre, Darius decided to launch his planned attack with the war chariots in order to decide the outcome of the battle before the horse Companions could swing to their left and attack his numerous infantry from the rear. The 200 Persian scythed chariots advanced rapidly, reaching the Macedonian front line at full speed and seeming set to break the ranks of the phalanxes. Alexander, however, had prepared his foot soldiers for such attack and they were ready to respond. As they neared the Macedonian lines, the Persian charioteers came under an intense rain of missiles from the elite light infantry of the Agrianes, who had been deployed in front of the phalangites under the protection of their long pikes. Many drivers of the attacking chariots were killed by the javelins of the Macedonian light infantry, with the result that the Persians lost most of their initial coordination. The foot Companions of the phalanxes then opened up their ranks in order to create alleys through which the scythed chariots could pass. Waiting for the charioteers at the end of these alleys were the hypaspists, the elite Macedonian light infantrymen attacking individual chariots from the rear once they had slowed down after breaking up their formations. It was then extremely easy for them to kill the Persian drivers and thereby neutralize all the war chariots. Alexander's tactic had worked perfectly and Darius had lost his crack shock troops without causing significant casualties to the enemy.

Soon after the Persian attack was repulsed, Alexander invested the Achaemenid centre with his horse Companions deployed in wedge formation. The Persian infantry were attacked on their left by the Macedonian cavalry, while the phalanxes (which had resumed their advance) smashed them from the front. It was at this crucial moment that Alexander secured victory: the Persian centre collapsed and he charged with the Companion cavalry against the position occupied by Darius. The Achaemenid king risked being killed or captured by the Macedonian cavalry, who came very near to his chariot, but the horse Companions were temporarily slowed by the strong resistance of the Immortals and the Greek mercenary hoplites, who gave Darius enough time to flee from the battlefield. Alexander was ready to closely pursue his defeated rival, capture him and kill the remaining Persian soldiers who were falling back in complete disorder. At this point, however, he received a desperate request for help from his left wing, which was commanded by Parmenion. The Persian cavalry had surrounded Parmenion's Macedonian troops and was on the verge of destroying them. The Achaemenid mounted troops were much more numerous than the Macedonian light cavalry facing them, and the whole left wing of Alexander's army was at risk of being crushed. Alexander had to make a very difficult decision: should he follow Darius and kill him in order to end the war, or should he return to save part of his army from destruction? In the end, he decided to turn back with his elite heavy cavalry, which routed the Persian mounted troops that had surrounded Parmenion. In the aftermath of the battle, the Macedonians occupied the enemy camp, where they captured the Persian war elephants as well as the Achaemenid

Scythian heavy cavalryman equipped with a full set of scale armour. The Chalcidian helmet is of Greek manufacture. (*Photo and copyright by Amages Drachen*)

Scythian heavy cavalryman; both his helmet and corselet are covered with metal scales. (*Photo and copyright by Scythian State*)

baggage train containing vast amounts of gold. Gaugamela had been a monumental triumph for Alexander, the Persian army having suffered a total of some 50,000 casualties, including all its best soldiers. For their part, the Macedonians lost only 1,500 or so men.

After defeating Darius III for a second time, Alexander invaded southern Mesopotamia and occupied Babylon. The Macedonians entered the city in triumph and discovered a new world: the fabulous city, famous for its gardens and religious buildings, had until that time been visited by just a few Greek merchants. The first of the four Persian capitals thus fell, and was soon followed by the second one, the magnificent city of Susa in Elam (on the eastern borders of modern Kuwait). Despite having been soundly defeated and lost two of his richest cities, Darius still had no intention of surrendering. He continued to exert control over the eastern half of the Persian Empire, which comprised the heartland of his people (Iran) and several other provinces stretching south to India and north to Central Asia. All these lands were inhabited by warlike peoples, so Darius could easily recruit another army from them. In addition, some Achaemenid troops had been able to escape from the battlefield of Gaugamela and had followed their monarch: 1,000 Bactrian cataphracts commanded by Bessus, half of the Immortals and some 2,000 Greek mercenaries. Differently from what had happened before, Darius now acted rapidly. He sent letters to all his eastern satraps, ordering them to mobilize their fighting forces, and gave a speech in front of his remaining soldiers in order to boost their morale. The Achaemenid king then moved to Ecbatana, in the Zagros Mountains of Iran, where he started putting together a new army. To mobilize a sufficient number of warriors and to organize them into an effective fighting force, however, Darius needed time: to gain some of this, he left behind 3,000 of his best soldiers with orders to slow down Alexander's movements as long as possible. These chosen soldiers were under the command of Ariobarzanes, one of the most experienced Persian generals. To enter Iran, the Macedonians had to march on the Royal Road, a Persian highway built several decades before by Darius I, which connected Susa with the two eastern capitals of the Achaemenids: Persepolis and Pasargadae. The terrain surrounding the Royal Road was covered by mountains, and marching across it during the winter months was extremely hazardous, especially to an army that had little knowledge of the region. The Zagros Mountains marked the border between Mesopotamia and Persia (Iran); only a few roads crossed them, and these all passed through narrow mountain passes. Ariobarzanes had extensive knowledge of these passes and could potentially defend them for months with his few elite troops to provide Darius with the time to raise and train a new army.

After conquering Susa, Alexander continued his advance by dividing his army into two parts: one, under the command of Parmenion, moved along the Royal Road, while the other, under his own orders, tried to cross the Zagros Mountains by traversing a narrow mountain pass known as the Persian Gate. This pass could be easily defended by a small number of men and was perfect for carrying out an ambush. During his advance, Alexander had to fight against some local tribes, such as the Uxians, who attacked him with hit-and-run tactics. Meanwhile, Ariobarzanes and his Persians prepared an ambush in the Persian Gate. The pass was preceded by a valley that was initially very wide but then progressively narrowed before reaching the Persian Gate. Realizing that the Macedonians were ignorant of much of the terrain, the Persians deployed on the two slopes surrounding the Persian Gate and built a wall to block the pass. At its narrowest point, the pass was just a couple of metres wide. Here the Persians ambushed Alexander and his men, who probably numbered less than 10,000. Ariobarzanes's plan worked perfectly, the Macedonians being caught unawares while crossing the Persian Gate and suffering severe

Scythian noble; note the rich decorations embroidered on his clothes and the use of a jewelled waist-belt. (*Photo and copyright by Scythian State*)

Scythian horse archer; the Scythians usually employed bright colours for the production of their clothes. (*Photo and copyright by Amages Drachen*)

losses as the Achaemenid soldiers attacked them with a rain of arrows and boulders. Alexander, finding his passage blocked, had no choice but to fall back in order to reorganize his forces. During the following four weeks, the Persians defended the mountain pass with great determination, like the Spartan hoplites who fought at Thermopylae during the Second Greco-Persian War. Ariobarzanes wanted to stop Alexander until the coming of spring and had all the resources to do so. However, the Macedonian king, well aware of the risks that he was running in the heart of the Zagros Mountains, finally decided to use one of his trademark tactics to get out of his predicament. He organized a complex pincer attack after sending some of his best light infantry to climb over the two hills that surrounded the Persian Gate. The defenders, taken by surprise, were crushed after some very bitter fighting. Ariobarzanes had been sure that the Macedonians would never find a path across the hills to attack his flanks. Apparently, however, Alexander was able to employ some Persian prisoners as guides and thereby found a way to encircle the Achaemenid soldiers. Although the Macedonians did seize the Persian Gate, it was only at the cost of heavy casualties. The defeat of Ariobarzanes removed the last military obstacle between Alexander and Persepolis, which was subsequently easily taken by the Macedonians, together with its treasury, considered to be the richest in the ancient world. The final capital of the Persian Empire, Pasargadae, also swiftly fell to Alexander's men. Surprised by Alexander's relatively quick victory at the Persian Gate, Darius had to abandon Ecbatana and moved east in order to continue mobilizing his troops. After the Macedonians prevailed at the Persian Gate, Darius went to the eastern satrapies of Bactria and Sogdia, which were ruled by the powerful governor Bessus. The latter had commanded the left wing of the Persian forces at the Battle of Gaugamela, which was mostly made up of skilled warriors from his satrapies who were mobilized after the Battle of Issus. Bessus had been able to survive the bloody clash at Gaugamela, together with part of his forces, after which he fled to Ecbatana with Darius and then the king when he decided to move further east. Darius planned to move to the satrapies of Central Asia, where he could raise another army and plan a counter-offensive against Alexander. With the end of winter, the Persians were closely pursued by the Macedonians, who wanted to capture Darius in order to finally bring the war to an end.

While fleeing to Bactria, with Alexander's cavalry hot on his heels, Bessus plotted against Darius with the other satraps of the Central Asian provinces. The conspiracy led to the Achaemenid monarch being put in golden chains by the traitors, who selfishly hoped that by giving their king to Alexander they could obtain some political advantage, such as retaining their personal possessions. The most ambitious of the traitors was Bessus, who wished to replace Darius as the supreme monarch of the

Scythian horse archer wearing his padded clothing (*trimmed with fur*) that was designed for winter use. (*Photo and copyright by Amages Drachen*)

Scythian horse archer armed with a deadly composite bow of the steppes.
(Photo and copyright by Somatophylaques)

Persians and probably hoped to secure control over the vast eastern provinces of the Achaemenid Empire. The rebel satraps tried to surrender the deposed king to the Macedonians, but Alexander would accept no agreement and ordered the chase of the remaining Persian forces to continue. At this point, Bessus and the other traitors stabbed Darius and left him dying in a chariot that was found by the pursuing Macedonians. Bessus immediately proclaimed himself King of Persia, adopting the name of Artaxerxes V. In many respects, his self-proclaimed ascension to the head of the empire was logical, since the Satrap of Bactria was the nearest noble to Darius's heirs in the line of succession to the Persian throne. When Alexander saw Darius's body, he ordered the enemy king to be buried with full honours and showed great respect to his former rival. He also vowed that he would severely punish Darius's killers. The death of Darius did not lead to the end of the war, which now continued between Alexander and Bessus. The Macedonians began their conquest of Central Asia that would eventually lead them into India. In 329 BC, the Macedonian army entered Bactria by way of the Hindu Kush mountain range, which had been left undefended by Bessus. The intentions of Bessus were simple: he wanted to move his forces further east in order to weaken the morale of the Macedonians and stretch their supply routes to breaking point. Having superior knowledge of the local terrain, he had in mind to conduct a guerrilla campaign against Alexander's forces. By causing continuous losses to the enemy with guerrilla tactics and burning crops while retreating, Bessus hoped to wear down and defeat the Macedonians while avoiding any direct confrontation with them. After crossing the Oxus River, which today marks the border between Afghanistan and Tajikistan, the Bactrian mounted troops deserted and abandoned Bessus, who was seized by some of his chieftains and handed over to the pursuing Macedonians. He was then tortured and killed as punishment for having dethroned the legitimate monarch, Darius III. Alexander thereby gained the support of several Persian nobles who were still loyal to the memory of Darius. The death of Bessus marked the effective end of the Achaemenid Empire. Alexander continued to campaign in the former Persian territories of Central Asia for several years, but there was no longer any central 'Persian' political authority to speak of. One of the greatest empires in the history of the world had disappeared forever.

Chapter 6

The Achaemenid Army

The main characteristic of the Persians' attitude to empire was a readiness to let their subject peoples maintain their own politico-military institutions when these did not conflict with Achaemenid rule. As a result, the various provinces of the immense Persian Empire all deployed military contingents that had their own distinctive features in terms of equipment and tactics. This made the Achaemenid army an extremely heterogeneous and multi-ethnic military force, whose components had different traditions and behaviours. As already mentioned, Darius I reorganized the administrative structure of the Persian Empire on twenty satrapies, or provinces, that were later increased to twenty-three: Persia, Media, Elam, Babylonia, Assyria, Arabia, Countries by the Sea (i.e. Cilicia, Phoenicia and Cyprus), Egypt, Lydia, Asia Minor (i.e. the Greek colonies), Cappadocia, Armenia, Parthia, Bactria, Sogdia, Scythia, Drangiana, Aria, Chorasmia, Arachosia, Maka, Sattagydia and Gandhara (the latter two being located in northern India). The society of the Achaemenid Empire could be described as a feudal one, since it comprised three main components: the aristocracy or *azata*, the commoners or *bandaka* and the slaves or *mariaka*. All the commoners were considered to be bondsmen of the monarch, and as such were required to perform compulsory military service. Exemption from such service was difficult to obtain, since it could only be granted by the king. Before his fifth year, a Persian boy was not admitted into the presence of his father and lived entirely with the women of his family. He then underwent fifteen years of low-intensity informal military training, during which he was taught how to ride and how to use the bow, before becoming part of the army for a period of four years at the age of 20. The young recruits were divided into small companies, each mustering fifty men, which were commanded by the sons of the landed nobility. After his four years of active service, a Persian commoner was demobilized, but he remained liable for military service until the age of 50. The various military units were organized as regiments mustering 1,000 men each, which were known as *hazarabam* or thousands. Each regiment was divided into ten *sataba* or hundreds, which were in turn subdivided into *dathaba* of ten men. Each *sataba* had an officer who acted as second-in-command and thus could be divided into two sections if needed. The decimal system of Persian units was also maintained for the raising of larger military

Scythian horse archer; note the large dimensions of both the bow and quiver. (*Photo and copyright by Amages Drachen*)

Scythian horse archer preparing his bow for battle. (*Photo and copyright by Scythian State*)

corps, such as divisions. To form a single division of 10,000 men, ten regiments were usually assembled together. The perfect organizational system described above, of course, was not always maintained, and in most cases the various units had internal establishments that were much smaller than planned.

All the officers of the Achaemenid army were Persians or Medes, while the common soldiers could come from every corner of the empire. The king commanded his troops only in case of major military campaigns, as it was common practice to appoint overall commanders from the most important families of the Persian or Median aristocracy in case of war. Local campaigns, taking place on the frontiers of the empire, were usually conducted by the satraps whose provinces were affected by the military operations. Each Achaemenid regiment had its own distinctive standard and was recruited from a specific area of the empire. According to sources, only

Scythian horse archer firing with his composite bow. (*Photo and copyright by Amages Drachen*)

the Persian and Median recruits underwent the kind of military training described above, the other peoples of the Achaemenid Empire having their own traditions. A fundamental component of the Persians' informal training was hunting, which accustomed the youths to physical exercise and the use of weapons. The Persian/Median aristocracy was extremely warlike and considered commanding military units one of its essential tasks. Consequently, it was vital for the Achaemenid monarchs to be able to count on the loyalty of their aristocrats in order to deploy effective fighting forces.

The Immortals

The core of the Achaemenid army was the famous royal guard of the Immortals, which consisted of 10,000 men, a full division mustering ten regiments of infantry. The Immortals were professional soldiers coming from the heartland of Persia who provided military service on a permanent basis. They responded directly to the monarch and underwent intensive training. The Immortals were renowned for their discipline and valour in battle, being the elite of the Persian military forces. They took part only in the most important expeditions, their presence being needed in the heart of the empire to prevent the outbreak of local revolts. Most of the Immortals' officers had personal links with the Achaemenid royal family, which made them extremely loyal. The name 'Immortals' derived from the fact that every member of the corps who was killed or wounded was immediately replaced with a new one in order to maintain the royal guard's division as a cohesive military unit with a constant strength. Presumably, the gaps in the ranks of the royal guardsmen were filled by men promoted from other units who had distinguished themselves for their valour. The royal guard, in addition to the troops performing garrison duties, was the only component of the Achaemenid army to be kept in service in peacetime. The royal guardsmen followed the monarch during his journeys around the empire and garrisoned his various residences. Most of the Immortals were Persians, but the royal guard also included Median and Elamite elements. Members of the elite corps were equipped as heavy infantrymen and were referred to as 'spear-bearers'. According to Herodotus, 1,000 of the Immortals – i.e. one regiment – had spears whose butts resembled golden pomegranates, while the remaining 9,000 – nine regiments – had spears with butts resembling silver pomegranates. It is possible that the 1,000 guardsmen with golden spear-butts were equipped with body shields and were tasked with protecting the other 9,000, who carried smaller shields and bows in addition to their spears. The most common tactical formation of the Achaemenid forces consisted of a screen of spearmen equipped with body shields, behind which sizeable numbers of archers could be deployed to fire their arrows. All the Immortals were classified as heavy infantry, so the 9,000 archers probably wore armour like the 1,000 spearmen. The practice of equipping archers with armour, shields and spears was adopted by the Persians from the Assyrians and was one of the main peculiarities of their military system.

In addition to the Immortals, the Achaemenid army also comprised some other guard corps that were specifically tasked with protecting the life of their monarch. These consisted of four regiments: one regiment of Persian infantry, one of Median infantry, one of Persian cavalry and one of Median cavalry. These units were probably

Scythian light infantryman equipped as a skirmisher. (*Photo and copyright by Scythian State*)

Thracian tribal warrior wearing a fur cap made from the skin of a fox and a pair of soft boots. (*Photo and copyright by Somatophylaques*)

Thracian peltast wearing winter clothes. (*Photo and copyright by Ancient Thrace*)

recruited from the best elements of the Immortals and many of their members were related to the Achaemenid royal family. According to Herodotus, the guardsmen of the two infantry regiments carried spears with butts that resembled golden apples, which distinguished them from the other Immortals. We know very little of the mounted guardsmen, but since they came from the most important aristocratic families of the empire it can be presume that they were heavily equipped.

On the march all the members of the Achaemenid royal guard – whether Immortals or not – carried their spears reversed in order to show their distinctive spear-butts. Each regiment was followed by a caravan of covered carriages, camels and mules that transported the guardsmen's supplies and attendants. The Immortals had the privilege of eating some special food that was reserved only for their consumption. While performing ceremonial service in the royal residences, the guardsmen wore a distinctive tiara and the Elamite robe. The tiara, resting on the long twisted horns of the Ethiopian ram, consisted of three bunches of reeds, each surmounted by a solar disc and set against a background of ostrich feathers. The Elamite robe was full-length and fringed. It passed over the right arm and was backed by a narrow border of rosettes on both the vertical and horizontal hems of the fringes. The decorative rosettes each had eight petals and eight minute sepals. According to contemporary sources, each regiment of the Immortals had its ceremonial robe in a different distinctive colour. On campaign, the rich Elamite robe was replaced with a standard long-sleeved tunic and trousers, which were worn together with corselets of scale armour. The tiara was substituted by a standard Persian cap made of cloth or felt, which resembled a hood and could be pulled over the face to keep out wind and dust. The ceremonial dress described above was commonly known as Persian dress, while the more practical one worn on campaign was called Median dress, the Persians having adopted it from the Medes. The ceremonial shields of the Immortals were figure-of-eight shaped and could be decorated with bronze elements. The shields used for combat were made of wicker covered with leather and could be of two different kinds: large rectangular shields covering the entire body of their bearer or smaller circular shields mostly designed to protect from enemy arrows. The royal guardsmen who were equipped as archers carried the standard Median bow – which was quite small and entirely made of wood – together with a quiver. The quiver could be of the Persian model (rectangular in shape and open, being made of wicker) or the Median model (cylindrical in shape and closed, being made of leather). The swords and daggers carried by the Immortals, as well as by most of the Achaemenid military forces, were of the akinakes type. They were 35–60cm in length and double-edged, having a straight blade and a guard that could be lobed (with the hilt resembling that of a bollock dagger, with two oval swellings) or have a pommel of the antenna type.

The scabbard of the akinakes swords or daggers was usually made of golden bronze and had a large decorative mount near the opening, in order to be suspended from a belt on the wearer's right side. Both the pommels and the scabbards of the akinakes could be richly decorated, for example with the reproduction of animal heads.

Persians and Medians

The Persians and Medians made up the bulk of the Achaemenid army, but except for those serving in the royal guard, most of them were part-time soldiers who were mobilized only in case of need. There were, however, some military contingents that served on a permanent basis also in peacetime: these were the bodyguards of the various satraps (which often consisted of mercenaries, who could be foreigners) and the garrison corps. These could be made up of professional soldiers recruited from the most warlike peoples of the Achaemenid Empire or of military colonists who received a grant of land from the monarch in exchange for performing military service. The practice of settling military colonists in frontier areas was initiated in the Middle East by the Neo-Babylonian Empire and was continued by the Achaemenids, who created several settlements of Persian and Median cavalrymen in the border areas of their vast empire. In several cases, the military colonists performed the task of collecting taxes, which was fundamental for the correct functioning of the Achaemenid military apparatus as garrison corps had to be paid on a regular basis in order to avoid the outbreak of revolts. Before the Greco-Persian Wars, the Achaemenid infantry from Persia and Media consisted of two categories of troops: heavily equipped *sparabara*, or shield-bearers, and archers. Each *dathaba* of the Achaemenid foot troops comprised one shield-bearer and nine archers. The *sparabara* were trained to form a shield wall on the battlefield, behind which the archers could deploy and fire their arrows. Each shield-bearer was equipped with a massive rectangular shield made of wicker covered with leather, along with a 2-metre-long spear. Nine rows of archers were deployed behind each shield-bearer, under a tactical practice that had been initiated – albeit with some differences – by the Assyrians. As a result of this, the firepower of the Persian and Median archers was the key element on which Achaemenid battle tactics were based. The practice worked extremely well during the campaigns fought in Asia, where most of the enemy infantry consisted of lightly equipped warriors who were extremely vulnerable to arrows. When the Achaemenid troops started to face the Greeks, however, the situation changed dramatically, the heavily equipped hoplites having bronze armour that could not be penetrated by the Persian or Median arrows. The *sparabara* wore quilted linen armour but no helmets, while the archers rarely had cuirasses but could sometimes carry a light spear in addition to their bow.

Thracian peltast wearing summer clothes. (*Photo and copyright by Ancient Thrace*)

Thracian peltast during a reconnaissance mission. (*Photo and copyright by Ancient Thrace*)

Thracian peltast guarding a defensive position. (*Photo and copyright by Ancient Thrace*)

Apparently, only the Immortals were armed with spear, bow and shield at the same time. Additionally, the royal guardsmen were the only foot soldiers to have iron scale armour, together with the officers who commanded the regular infantry units. Before the Greco-Persian Wars, the Persian and Median cavalry of the Achaemenid army consisted of lightly armed horsemen who were equipped with throwing javelins and bows. Very few of the cavalrymen wore helmets of hammered bronze or iron, and cuirasses of quilted linen were only rarely worn. Before overcoming the Medes, the Persians did not have a very large or effective cavalry arm, so a good number of the Achaemenid mounted troops consisted of Median horsemen.

Following their experience of combat in the Greco-Persian Wars, the Achaemenid foot troops started to modify their standard equipment so they would be better prepared to face the Greek hoplites on the field of battle. The previous tactical organization based on the co-existence of *sparabara* and archers was abandoned, with most of the foot soldiers starting to be equipped with crescent-shaped pelte shields and javelins. The pelte shield was the most distinctive element of Thracian warriors' traditional panoply (see below) and had already been adopted by the Greek light infantry peltasts before the outbreak of the Greco-Persian Wars. The new Persian and Median infantry equipped with pelte shield and throwing javelins became known as *takabara*, often adding a short axe to their offensive weapons and being capable of fighting hand-to-hand if needed. Over time, however, it became apparent that even the introduction of the new *takabara* units had not resolved the many problems experienced by the Achaemenid foot troops when facing the Greek hoplites. The hoplites were well protected against the javelins thrown by the Persian and Median infantry and could kill their opponents from distance thanks to their long spears. Consequently, the Achaemenid rulers had no choice but to recruit increasing numbers of Greek mercenary hoplites for their armies. Around 370 BC, the Achaemenids started to develop their own type of hoplites, retraining as heavy infantry some of the Persian/Median foot soldiers, who received the new denomination of *kardakes*. By the time of Alexander the Great's invasion of the Achaemenid Empire, there were some 20,000 *kardakes*, equipped with round shields that were almost identical to those carried by the Greek hoplites. The *kardakes*, however, had shorter spears than the Hellenic heavy infantrymen and usually did not wear any kind of armour. The creation of the *kardakes* was probably just the first step in a more general reform of the Achaemenid infantry, which was unable to be completed due to the Macedonian invasion of the Persian Empire. It is important to note that – during the whole period covered in this volume – the Achaemenid infantry always included sizeable numbers of lightly equipped slingers who supported the archers in performing their usual tactical functions. After the Greco-Persian Wars, the Achaemenid cavalry was also progressively re-equipped. Most of the Persian/Median horsemen started to be armed only with cornel-wood heavy javelins that were designed for throwing. In addition, the Achaemenids began to develop their own form of heavy cavalry by copying those of the Bactrians and Sogdians. The new heavy cavalry were equipped with bronze helmets, cuirasses (consisting of iron scales or made from quilted linen) and thrusting spears. Furthermore, horse armour (*parapleuridia*) started to be used, consisting of thigh-protectors and flank-protectors made of bronze that also served as thigh-pieces for the riders. The *parapleuridia* were attached to the saddle and were made of bronze scales that were applied on a cloth or leather backing. The cavalrymen of the royal guard and the satraps' mounted bodyguards were all heavily equipped. During the whole of this period, the Persian and Median cavalry was never equipped with shields. The Achaemenid cavalry was supported by a number of scythed chariots, each of which was drawn by four horses. War chariots had been an important component of the Assyrian and Babylonian military forces for several centuries, but they lost most of their previous tactical functions under the Achaemenids as they proved to be of no use against the Greek heavy infantry deployed in close formation.

Kissians, Babylonians and Assyrians

The Kissians lived in the region of the Zagros Mountains and around Susa, in the very heartland of the Achaemenid Empire. They were a people of Elamite stock, but over time they adopted many cultural features of the Persians, who lived very near to their home territories. The Kissians, according to Herodotus, were wilder than the Persians but fought exactly like them. In particular, they provided infantry units of *sparabara* and archers. Kissian warriors could be distinguished from those of the Persians and Medes because they wore a mitre cap and a knotted headband instead of the usual Persian/Median headgear. Kissian archers were armed with the standard wooden bow of the Achaemenid armies, which was originally designed by the Medes. Assyria and Babylonia, which had once been dominant powers of the Middle East, provided sizeable military contingents to the Persians. These were frequently brigaded together, consisting of Assyrian heavy infantrymen equipped with body shields and of Babylonian archers. Most of the Assyrian and Babylonian foot soldiers wore pointed metal helmets and corselets of iron scale armour, which made them heavily equipped, which was quite uncommon by contemporary Achaemenid standards.

Phoenicians, Jews and Arabs

Phoenicia, together with Egypt and the Greek cities of Asia Minor, provided the bulk of the Persian navy's marines. The Phoenician naval infantrymen were considered

Thracian peltast ready to throw one of his javelins. (*Photo and copyright by Ancient Thrace*)

Thracian warlord armed with a kopis sword. (*Photo and copyright by Ancient Thrace*)

Thracian warrior armed with a sickle dagger. (*Photo and copyright by Ancient Thrace*)

the best in the Mediterranean world. They wore crested helmets made of bronze that were similar to contemporary Greek ones, as well as cuirasses made of leather or linen. Most of the Phoenician marines carried round shields with bronze rims and were armed with harpoons in addition to their throwing javelins, the Phoenician naval infantry being specialized in boarding enemy warships. The Jews did not provide significant military contingents to the Achaemenid army, but did supply some units of lightly equipped archers that were mostly employed by the Persians as garrison troops. The warlike Arab tribes living between Mesopotamia and Egypt were formally allies of the Achaemenids and thus provided them with auxiliary military contingents. These consisted of foot or camel-mounted archers, who were armed with backward-curving bows and wore no kind of personal protection.

Armenians, Cappadocians and Paphlagonians

The Armenians and Cappadocians provided excellent mountain infantry to the Persians, which comprised lightly equipped skirmishers armed with throwing javelins who defended themselves with small round shields. The Paphlagonians provided the same kind of light infantry as well as some light cavalry contingents, whose members were equipped with leather helmets and throwing javelins.

Cilicians, Lycians and Carians

The Cilicians, Lycians and Carians all provided both marines and light infantry units to the Persians. The naval infantrymen were equipped similarly to the Greek hoplites, with bronze helmets and cuirasses, but also carried hoplon round shields and were often armed with forked spears or harpoons. The most distinctive offensive weapon of these Anatolian warriors, however, was the drepanon reaping hook, a form of sickle sword that was specifically designed for naval combat.

Phrygians and Lydians

The Phrygians were mostly equipped like their Thracian 'cousins', having emerged from some Thracian tribal communities that had settled in Anatolia. In addition to the usual light infantry peltasts, however, the Phrygians also deployed some effective contingents of heavy cavalry, whose members wore corselets of bronze scale armour and bronze crested helmets having the distinctive shape of the famous Phrygian cap. The Phrygian heavy cavalrymen were usually armed with short axes or throwing javelins. The Lydian infantrymen were re-equipped as hoplites by King Croesus, who had a high opinion of the heavy infantry contingents deployed by the Greek cities of Asia Minor. As a result, they wore bronze helmets and cuirasses copied from those of the Greek hoplites, and carried round hoplon shields.

Scythians, Sogdians and Bactrians

The Scythians, called Saka by the Persians, had frequent interactions with the Achaemenid Empire despite not being part of it. They lived over a vast area of the Eurasian steppes, extending from Ukraine in the west to Mongolia in the east. The Persians also considered some other steppe peoples – like the Massagetae – who were ethnically distinct from them, to be part of the Scythians. Achaemenid military commanders had a high opinion of the Scythian cavalry, especially those having heavy equipment, so during several of the major campaigns fought by the Persians, the Achaemenid army deployed sizeable numbers of Scythian allies and mercenaries. Scythian warriors, like those of all the other nomadic peoples of the Eurasian steppes, mostly consisted of cavalry. Indeed, the Scythians were known as the best horse breeders of the world during Antiquity. The formidable Scythian cavalry had two main components: horse archers and heavy horsemen. The horse archers were mere much more numerous than the heavy cavalry, since every able-bodied Scythian male was capable of fighting as a mounted archer. They wore no armour and were equipped with the deadly composite bow of the Eurasian steppes. Whereas the Scythian commoners made up the light cavalry of the horse archers, the heavy cavalry consisted of noble professional warriors who were rich enough to equip themselves with a full panoply of armour. Broadly speaking, each heavy cavalry contingent was commanded by a prince and consisted of his armed retinue. The professional warriors of the heavy cavalry were used to fight in closed formation and thus were more disciplined than the horse archers, being elite shock troops. Scythian battle tactics were quite simple but worked extremely well in the steppes. They had evolved from the movements made by the Scythians while moving their herds of horses and cattle over vast plains, movements that had one main objective: concentrating the dispersed animals in a single point of the steppe in order to move them towards new areas of pasture. The battles of the steppe peoples were extremely rapid and violent, beginning with massive attacks by horse archers, who concentrated their volleys on the flanks of the enemy in order to oblige them to concentrate their forces in the centre. When the enemy had been manoeuvred into a single point of the battlefield, the heavily armoured cavalry launched a decisive frontal charge that usually won the day. These tactics worked perfectly against enemies with cavalry armies but were not always effective against opponents who could deploy large heavy infantry contingents (like the Greek hoplites or Macedonian phalangites). The Scythian cavalry was famous for its great tactical flexibility, being capable of regrouping in the thick of the action and changing direction very rapidly in order to strike where needed. When an enemy formation had been broken by the heavy cavalry, the horse archers pursued the defeated opponents in order to transform their retreat into a rout. The standard armour worn by most Scythian warriors consisted of flexible leather corselets that were partly or entirely covered with overlapping scales of bronze or iron. The Scythians were masters at producing bronze scale armour, also frequently reinforcing their helmets and shields by applying bronze or iron scales on their external surface. Scythian armourers cut the scales from sheet metal with a pointed tool or shears, and the scales were then attached to the soft leather base of the corselets by thin leather thongs or animal tendons. Each scale was set in such a way that it covered between a third and a half of the width of the next scale sideways. Each row of scales overlapped the one placed below it, protecting the stitching where it was exposed in holes through the metal. Despite providing excellent protection to their wearers, the corselets did not significantly hinder the movements of a mounted warrior. Various types of corselets were used, according to the economic capabilities of their wearers, the simplest and cheapest ones having metal scales only around the neck and upper breast or just on the front surface. Short-sleeved corselets were used by the common warriors, while nobles often had long-sleeved corselets. Frequently, a doubled yoke of scale-work was applied across the upper back and extending forward over the shoulders to the sides of the breast, in order to offer better protection for the shoulders. Sometimes the scales of a single corselet could be made from two different materials, in order to look even more magnificent, with polished bronze scales glittering in the sun against the lustreless iron scales. Scythian kings and princes could have corselets entirely covered with golden scales.

The early helmets of the Scythians were of the Kuban type, heavy cast-bronze helms, fitting tightly to the skull and protecting it way down the face by means of cheek-pieces that left cut-outs for the eyes. From the fifth century BC, the Kuban helmet started to be replaced by the new Phrygian one, a forward-pointing Phrygian cap made of leather and covered with metal scales. The Phrygian cap was extremely popular in the Balkans and was worn by most of the Thracian tribes, so it is highly probable that the Scythians started wearing it after coming into contact with the Thracians. Phrygian helmets could sometimes have cheek-pieces and neck-guards, always made of leather covered with metal scales. Being easy and cheap to produce, the Phrygian helmets were also used by the majority of the common Scythian warriors. Scythian noblemen gradually started to purchase increasingly large numbers of bronze helmets from the merchants of the Greek colonies in Crimea. These, according to

Mercenary Greek hoplite wearing a Chalcidian helmet and muscle cuirass. (*Photo and copyright by Somatophylaques*)

Mercenary Greek hoplite equipped with muscle cuirass that has some coloured decorative elements. (*Photo and copyright by Somatophylaques*)

Mercenary Greek hoplite wearing a linothorax cuirass that is reinforced by bronze scales on the front. (*Photo and copyright by Somatophylaques*)

recent findings, were mostly worn by the Scythian heavy cavalry and could be of three Hellenic models: Corinthian, Chalcidian or Attic. The defensive equipment of a Scythian noble warrior often included leg protection, which could be made of leather covered with scales or could consist of bronze greaves purchased in the Greek colonies of Crimea. Leggings covered with bronze or iron scales were a distinctive element of the Scythian heavy cavalry's panoply. The Greek-style bronze greaves of the richest individuals could be gilded and have decorative incisions. Both the helmets and the greaves purchased from the Greek merchants were part of the hoplites' heavy infantry equipment, but the Scythians adapted them to their traditional defensive panoply. The poorest Scythian warriors, fighting as light horsemen, had simple shields constructed from woven osiers, but the noble warriors carried massive shields faced with iron. The latter were constructed from a wooden base that was covered with scales of iron, which were sewn to each other and to the backing with wire. Kings and princes could occasionally have shields covered with a single iron plate, being decorated with applied motifs made from other metals. Deer and panther were the wild animals most frequently represented in Scythian decorations. Scythian shields were usually rectangular with curved angles, but sometimes could be crescent-shaped like those of the Thracians. The poorest Scythian warriors wore only a girdle for protection of their body. This was made of leather covered with metal scales, being broad enough to cover the whole abdomen. The armour worn by the horses of the Scythian heavy cavalry evolved considerably across the centuries. Initially it consisted just of metal plates and pendant decorations attached to the bridle for protection of the horse's head, but over time, pieces of leather horse-cloth covered with metal scales were introduced and became increasingly popular. A thick felt apron for the horse's breast was also developed, in order to provide better protection against enemy arrows. The Scythians, like all the other steppe peoples of Antiquity, rode without stirrups but were masters in the production of effective bridles. These were often decorated with bronze discs or plates. Scythian saddles were quite flat and simple, being manufactured from leather.

Every Scythian man had a composite bow and arrows, the bow being the 'national' weapon of the Scythians and all the nomadic warriors of the steppes. Contemporary written sources describe the Scythian composite bows as being unstrung and recurved. Their overall shape resembled that of the Greek letter *sigma* or the crescent moon with both ends curved inwards. The Scythian bow was quite short – about 80cm – but extremely powerful thanks to its composite construction. The composite bow was made from horn, wood and sinew laminated together. The horn was on the belly facing the archer, while sinew was on the outer side of the wooden core. The wooden core gave the bow its shape and stability. When the bow was drawn, the sinew (stretched on the outside) and horn (compressed on the inside) stored more energy than the wood for the same length of bow. The construction of a composite bow was a very complex process, requiring more varieties of material than a wooden bow and much more time. It was often made of multiple pieces, joined with animal glue in V-splices. Pieced construction allowed the use of woods with different mechanical properties for the bending and non-bending sections: the wood of the bending part of the limb had to endure intense shearing stress. A thin layer of horn was glued onto what would be the belly of the bow, which could store more energy than wood in compression. Goat or sheep horn was commonly used for this purpose. The sinew, soaked in animal glue, was then laid in layers on the back of the bow, the strands of sinew oriented along the length of the bow. The sinew was normally obtained from the lower legs and back of wild deer or domestic ungulates. Sinew would extend farther than wood, again allowing more energy storage. Hide glue was used to attach layers of sinew to the back of the bow and to fix the horn belly to the wooden core. The animal glue could lose strength in humid conditions and be quickly ruined by submersion or rain, so composite bows were always stored in protective leather cases. Historically, peoples living in humid or rainy regions have favoured wooden bows, while those living in dry or arid areas have preferred composite ones. The main advantage of composite bows over longbows was their combination of smaller size with high power. In addition, composite bows are recurved, as their shape curves away from the archer. This design gives them higher draw-weight in the early stages of the archer's draw, thus storing more total energy. The string of the Scythian bows was made from horsehair or animal tendon. Each bow was carried in a special case slung from the waist-belt, made of leather. This case, known as a *gorytos* and often being covered with metal plates on the external surface, also contained up to seventy-five arrows. As a result, it worked both as a case for the bow and as a quiver for the arrows. The shaft of the arrows was made from reed or a thin birch branch, while the fletching was made from birds' feathers. The heads of the arrows were of bronze or iron and had different shapes according to the use that the archer had to make of them. The standard arrows employed for fighting had trilobate heads that were capable of piercing enemy armour from long distances thanks to their excellent aerodynamic form. Scythian archers were capable of firing between ten and twelve arrows in a minute and could hit a target at a distance of 500 metres.

The earliest Scythian swords had a two-edged and almost parallel-sided blade tapering at the point. The blade was 60–70cm long. Daggers, having the same basic features and being employed as secondary weapons, had blades 35–40cm in length. The early Scythian swords were decorated with thin gold plates fixed round the hilt. Over time, Scythian swords changed the shape of their blades, which became that

Mercenary Greek hoplite equipped with Chalcidian helmet and linothorax.
(*Photo and copyright by Somatophylaques*)

Mercenary Greek hoplite wearing a cuirass made of hardened leather.
(Photo and copyright by Somatophylaques)

Mercenary Greek hoplite equipped with a Corinthian helmet and linothorax.
(*Photo and copyright by Somatophylaques*)

of an elongated isosceles triangle with a continuous taper down its whole length. During the fourth century BC, single-edged versions of this new kind of blade started to be produced. The pommel of the Scythian swords, which had a simple crossbar shape in the early models, gradually changed to have a more complex fashion with two talons of iron rising and curling inwards. The grip, initially having a cylindrical shape, gradually came to have a double-tapered or oval shape that was practical for combat use. The guard evolved to have a triangular shape, with a sharp and curved indent in the centre of its bottom edge. The scabbards of the Scythian swords were made of wood covered with leather and hung from the waist-belt by a thong passing through its projecting ear. The Scythian horsemen used different kinds of spears, according to the tactical function that they had to perform on the battlefield. The heavy cavalrymen were equipped with long spears of the kontus type. This was about 4 metres long and had to be wielded with two hands while directing the horse using the knees, making it a specialist weapon that required a lot of training and good horsemanship to use. The kontus was reputedly a weapon of great power, especially compared to other cavalry spears of its time. The great length of this deadly weapon was probably the origin of its name, since the Greek word '*kontus*' meant an oar or barge pole. The heavy cavalrymen who formed the personal retinue of a Scythian prince and wore full armour were usually armed with the kontus, which was employed as a shock weapon during frontal charges. Shorter spears, about 1.7–1.8 metres long, were used for throwing and thrusting. These weapons had leaf-shaped heads with a central spine as well as a socket for the wooden shaft. Scythian light cavalrymen carried throwing javelins instead of the spears described above. These had a long iron shank with a small pyramidal head, which was sharply barbed and designed to pierce an enemy shield. The Scythians, in addition to swords, also carried other weapons for hand-to-hand fighting, including battleaxes and maces. The axes had iron blades that could be richly decorated, while the maces had lobed heads and were also used as symbols of authority.

Sogdia and Bactria both provided light infantry contingents to the Persians made up of javelineers and archers, whose members were equipped similarly to the Medians. However, the two Central Asian satrapies were famed for their excellent cavalry. These comprised both lightly equipped mounted archers and heavily equipped cavalrymen. Generally speaking, the Sogdian and Bactrian horsemen looked very similar to the Scythian cavalry. According to contemporary sources, however, Sogdian and Bactrian heavy cavalry were 'heavier' than the Scythian version because they widely employed effective horse armour made of metal scales. Thanks to their long kontus spears, the heavily equipped horsemen from Sogdia and Bactria were the only cavalrymen of the Achaemenid army who could face the Macedonian horse Companions on almost

Mercenary Greek hoplite wearing a Chalcidian helmet and coloured linothorax. (*Photo and copyright by Somatophylaques*)

Mercenary Greek hoplite; he is unarmoured but wears a bronze helmet.
(Photo and copyright by Somatophylaques)

Mercenary Greek peltast equipped with crescent-shaped pelte shield. (*Photo and copyright by Somatophylaques*)

equal terms, as they showed at the Battle of Gaugamela when under the command of Bessus. It should be noted, however, that the Sogdian and Bactrian heavy cavalry were never particularly numerous because producing their complex defensive equipment was extremely costly.

Thracians

Thrace was controlled by the Persians for only a short period of time, but sizeable numbers of Thracian mercenary warriors were recruited, quite often by the satraps of Anatolia. As a result, the Thracians, who were called Skudra by the Persians, always remained a significant component of the Achaemenid military forces. By the beginning of the eighth century BC, the Thracians could already be considered one of the most flourishing peoples of Europe. They occupied a vast Balkan area south of the Danube and had established firm control over a significant part of Anatolia (consisting of the regions of Phrygia and Bithynia, which became Asian kingdoms over time but whose populations never lost their original Thracian culture). The Thracians of Europe, however, did not develop any form of unified kingdom for a long time. They were divided into more than forty tribes, which were constantly at war with each other. Indeed, Thracian society was an extremely warlike one, in which combat was considered one of the most important elements of a man's ordinary life. From an economic point of view, the Thracians practiced animal breeding much more than agriculture, the great majority of them being shepherds who lived off the products obtained from their sheep and goats. Inter-tribal skirmishes and raids were usually sparked by disputes among shepherds for control of their pastures. The majority of the Thracians did not live in permanent settlements, instead following their herds during most of the year. Thrace thus did not have any major city. Raiding the village of a rival tribe was a normal activity for a semi-nomad Thracian community, skirmishes and small localized wars being a great occasion to enlarge herds by capturing sheep and goats from an enemy. The territory of Thrace, mostly covered by hills, was not well suited to armies equipped with heavy equipment and moving in close formation. The only way to move rapidly and fight effectively in Thrace was to act as skirmishers, equipped with throwing weapons and trained in light infantry tactics. The territory of present-day Bulgaria (ancient Thrace), however, also comprises some plains where the Thracians could breed horses and where excellent cavalry contingents could be raised. The Thracian tribes were distinguished as either mountain or plain communities, according to the morphology of the hills or valleys on which they lived. According to ancient authors like Herodotus, the Thracians were the most numerous people of Europe: if united into a single kingdom, they

Egyptian naval infantryman equipped with padded helmet and cuirass as well as body shield. (*Colour plate by Patricio Greve Moller, copyright of Gabriele Esposito*)

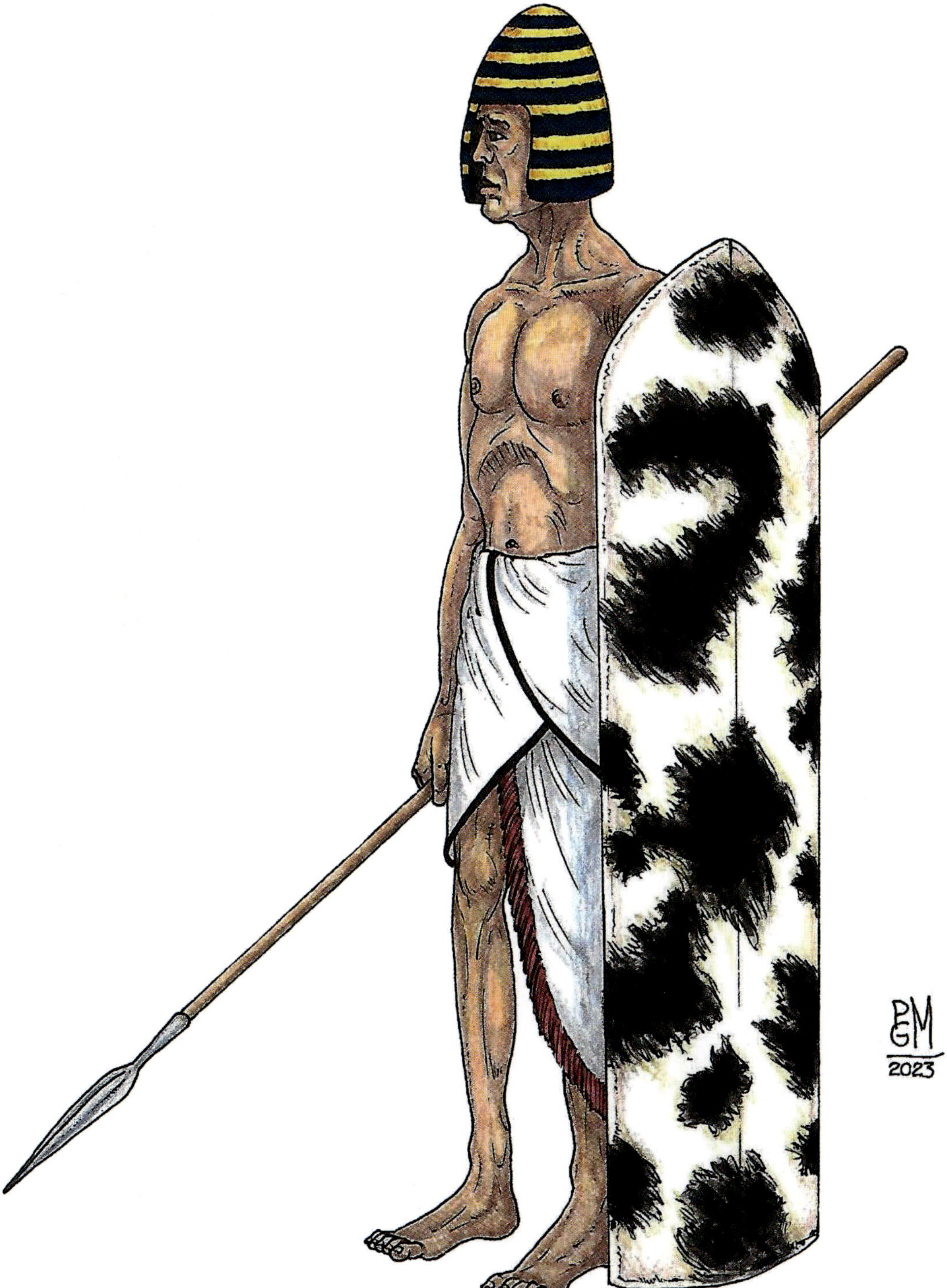

Egyptian infantryman carrying a spear and body shield.
(*Colour plate by Patricio Greve Moller, copyright of Gabriele Esposito*)

could have defeated and conquered all the ancient nations living along their borders. Luckily for their neighbours, however, the Thracians always preferred inter-tribal warfare to invasions directed against foreign peoples. Potentially, thanks to their great military capabilities, they could have been one of the leading powers of Antiquity.

By the end of the Greek Dark Ages, around 650 BC, the Thracians were already famed throughout the Mediterranean world for their combat skills and unrivalled courage on the battlefield, and thus started to be employed on a large scale as mercenaries by several ancient kingdoms. In Thrace, the profession of warrior was highly regarded, being considered superior to all other ways of life. Showing courage in battle was fundamental for a Thracian man to acquire a positive personal reputation. Generally speaking, however, Thracian warriors were not well-known for their martial discipline: they loved plunder more than anything else, which frequently caused them serious problems during a battle or campaign. The Thracians obeyed only strong war leaders who came from their own tribes, it being particularly difficult for foreign commanders to secure their loyalty. When serving as mercenaries, if not paid properly and on time, they were prone to mutinies and revolts. It was not uncommon for them to join the enemy

Egyptian archer wearing a well-manufactured corselet of scale armour. (*Colour plate by Patricio Greve Moller, copyright of Gabriele Esposito*)

if an opponent's leader offered them large amounts of gold or a good opportunity to plunder a rich city. The Thracians never lost their original character of semi-nomadic raiders, even after centuries of close contact with the major civilizations of the Mediterranean. Nothing was more important for them than personal wealth, and every possible method to augment this was considered to be legitimate. Well known for their cruelty, they were also famous for being high-spirited, with singing and dancing being two fundamental components of their daily life, together with drinking wine in large quantities. It should be pointed out, however, that their way of life was not so different from that of many other ancient peoples and that their technological skills were by no means rudimentary. They were able to produce deadly weapons with metals, as well as working tools. Although the Thracians were not used to living in urban centres or practicing commerce on a large scale, their simple economy was able to cause frequent demographical booms.

The standard 'national' costume of Thracian warriors comprised the following four basic elements: a tunic, cloak (*zeira*), cap (*alopekis*) and pair of boots (*embades*). Tunics and cloaks were produced in bright colours, a distinctive feature of Thracian dress, and they were usually decorated with geometrical patterns, which could be highly intricate. The quality of the tunic and cloak varied according to the economic possibilities of each warrior. According to ancient sources, Thracian tunics and cloaks were appreciated for their excellent texture: they were made of hemp, flax or wool. Some differences existed between the traditional costume worn by northern Thracians and that used by those who lived further south. In the north of Thrace, narrow trousers and a short shirt were added to the tunic and cloak in order to have better protection from cold temperatures. During winter months, especially in hilly regions, a fur cloak was usually worn over the standard *zeira*. Tunics were fastened with leather or textile belts, which could be richly decorated with metal elements. The traditional Thracian cap could be produced in three main versions: the first was made from a fox's skin and had the mask perched above the wearer's forehead, and comprised flaps of patterned cloth on the neck and on the cheeks. The second type was low-crowned and made of cloth or felt, while the third was high-crowned and had the classical shape of what became known as the Phrygian cap. These were produced in one piece, including the flaps covering the neck and cheeks. According to ancient sources, the first version was the most popular one, the fox being a sacred animal for the traditional religion of the Thracians. Among the tribes of northern Thrace, wearing the *alopekis* was a mark of social distinction and only the nobles were permitted to do it. Consequently, most of the ordinary warriors had no cap. The basic Thracian tunic was knee-length and sleeveless, being tied around the waist by a belt (the boss of which could be heavily decorated). The cloak covered the whole body, but without hampering movement. It was manufactured from heavy material and thus was quite stiff. The standard Thracian cloak reached the ankles and was perfect for protecting the body from cold temperatures during winter months. Its top portion could be folded over and its top corners could be turned in to hang over the chest or be thrown back over the shoulders. The cloak was held in place by a single brooch on the left shoulder. The traditional Thracian boots, the *embades*, were made from fawn-skin and covered the lower part of the leg as well as the whole feet. They were laced at the front, with some flaps (usually three) hanging down from the top. These boots were ideal for running over rocky terrain (also in snow) and were also worn by Thracian cavalrymen.

The basic equipment of a Thracian warrior was that of a light infantryman and always comprised a pelte shield and two javelins. The pelte was crescent-shaped in order to allow the throwing of javelins. Each Thracian light infantryman, or peltast, could throw a javelin from the top of the shield's convex part while protecting his torso behind the concave section. The pelte did not have a rim or any kind of metal facing; it was made of wicker or wood and was covered with goatskin or sheepskin. The

Nubian archer. The Nubians, living south of Egypt in present-day Sudan, were famous for the quality of their bowmen during Antiquity. (*Colour plate by Patricio Greve Moller, copyright of Gabriele Esposito*)

Thracian shield was usually carried with an arm strap and with a handle at the rim; it could also be transported on the back, being slung thanks to a back strap. On the back of the shield was a simple central grip. Generally speaking, the pelte was key to the tactical success of the peltasts. Thanks to this small but versatile shield, Thracian warriors had a great advantage over enemy light infantrymen who did not carry any form of body protection. It was light to transport and could also be employed by horsemen. As well as being designed for a fighter who threw javelins, it was perfectly suited to protect its user from enemy arrows. Thracian javelins had a very simple blade made of metal and were 1–1.5 metres in length. They were heavier and longer than the usual javelins carried by the Greek light infantry, so each Thracian warrior carried just a couple of them. According to ancient sources, the Thracians were masters at using their throwing weapons, able to hit the enemy from long distances and with incredible accuracy. This was the result of daily training and constant exercise. Prior to the third century BC, not all Thracian peltasts were armed with a couple of javelins, some of them being equipped with a 3-metre-long spear. This spear was obviously designed for close combat and not as a throwing weapon. The presence of some warriors armed with spear was an important element of Thracian tactics, especially after clashes with the Greeks became more frequent. Those fighters armed with spears acted as a screen for their companions equipped only with javelins. In case of an enemy counter-attack or defeat, the warriors equipped with spears could protect the retreat of the peltasts, who became particularly vulnerable after throwing both their javelins. Spearmen were not organized into separate groups, but a certain number of them were usually mixed among the standard peltasts. They were of great use when the peltasts were charged by enemy cavalry or when a formation of hoplites came too close to them. All Thracian warriors were equipped with a simple knife that had a curved blade, which could be a deadly weapon close combat. The Thracians had another deadly weapon in their traditional panoply, the Rhomphaia. This was a two-handed cutting weapon similar to a sickle, with a long blade that could be straight or slightly curved and was single-edged. The Rhomphaia was almost entirely made of iron, having just a wooden or bone grip covering the tang of the handle. The blade had an overall length of 50–60cm, making it particularly deadly. The Rhomphaia was perfect to hamstring horses and thus was an excellent weapon against cavalry, and it could also easily sever a human head from its body. During the Hellenistic period, when the Thracian peltasts gradually transformed into medium infantry, an increasing number of them substituted their javelins with a Rhomphaia. It was quite heavy to transport, meaning only the strongest warriors were usually equipped with it. As a weapon for hand-to-hand fighting it was particularly feared, since it could easily kill even an armoured soldier with just a single blow.

Ethiopian infantryman. Most Ethiopian warriors were armed with primitive offensive weapons such as clubs. (*Colour plate by Patricio Greve Moller, copyright of Gabriele Esposito*)

Ethiopian archer. During Antiquity, Ethiopian warriors were famed for painting their bodies white and red. (*Colour plate by Patricio Greve Moller, copyright of Gabriele Esposito*)

Greeks

The Greeks from the colonies of Asia Minor served in the Achaemenid army mostly as naval hoplites, but their military contribution was never a particularly significant one as their loyalty towards the Persian monarchs was quite dubious. The Persians employed sizeable numbers of Greek mercenary hoplites within their military forces after the end of the Greco-Persian Wars, when they badly needed some well-trained contingents of heavy infantry. The presence of Greek mercenaries was more significant in the western satrapies of the empire and remained extremely important until the Macedonian invasion. After the end of the Peloponnesian War that pitched Athens against Sparta between 431 and 404 BC, it became increasingly difficult for the various Greek cities to assemble large numbers of citizen-soldiers, most of them starting to consider their temporary employment as soldiers as a form of punishment. The original spirit of the hoplite, which linked military duties to political representation, was gradually disappearing. In addition, the new form of 'total warfare' experienced by Athens and Sparta during the Peloponnesian War required professional full-time soldiers who could fight in every season of the year and could train regularly. Consequently, most of the Greek *poleis* started to hire substantial numbers of mercenary hoplites to replace their part-time fighters. Generally speaking, mercenary hoplites came from the poorest areas of Greece, such as Achaea or Arcadia, regions that had very few natural resources and where the terrain was not particularly suitable for agriculture (being covered with hills or mountains). As a result, enlisting as a mercenary was the only chance to earn a living for most of the young males from Achaea and Arcadia.

The heavy infantry contingents of the mercenary hoplites were organized into regiments, or *taxeis*, which were in turn divided into companies, or *lochoi*. The number of soldiers making up each *taxis* widely varied, but a single regiment usually comprised 1,000 men from ten *lochoi*, each *lochos* generally having 100 hoplites. Following the end of the Greco-Persian Wars, the internal organization of the *lochoi* became more complex: each company was divided into two *pentekostyes* of fifty men each, which were in turn split into two *enomotia*, each of twenty-five men. At the beginning of the fourth century BC, an innovative general named Iphicrates, who had served the Persians as a mercenary commander, reformed the traditional Greek infantry by changing the standard panoply of the hoplites and peltasts. Iphicrates was the first who saw the great potential of the peltasts as medium infantry, which could fight both as light skirmishers and heavy shock troops according to circumstances. In 391 BC, at the Battle of Lechaeum, he was able to defeat a contingent of Spartan hoplites with just a force of Athenian peltasts for the first time in history. During the

Libyan archer. Libyan tribal warriors from the western frontier of Egypt were mostly equipped as unarmoured bowmen. The cloak, made from the skin of a cow, offered some protection against enemy arrows. (*Colour plate by Patricio Greve Moller, copyright of Gabriele Esposito*)

Indian noble. Wearing helmets and cuirasses made of bronze, they usually fought from the top of their war elephants. (*Colour plate by Patricio Greve Moller, copyright of Gabriele Esposito*)

previous years, he had already modified the panoply and tactics of the Athenian peltasts: instead of the traditional pelte shield, Iphicrates gave them a large oval shield made of wicker, while the new peltasts wore a helmet for protection of the head. Offensive weapons now also included a short sword and a short spear, in addition to the usual javelins. Thanks to the larger shield and new helmet, the Iphicratean peltast could fight in close order against a hoplite, while the new sword and spear meant he had more or less the same offensive capabilities as a heavy infantryman. Compared to a hoplite, however, the new peltast was much more mobile since he wore no armour. In practice, Iphicrates had completed the transition of the peltast from a light infantryman to a medium one. After the success at Lechaeum, the Athenian general decided to modify the panoply and tactics of the standard hoplite too. The large hoplon shield was abandoned in favour of a much smaller and lighter round shield, while the metal greaves were discarded and replaced by new comfortable leather boots known as Iphicratids, from the name of their creator. New lighter cuirasses made of quilted linen replaced the older models, and the spear, to compensate for the lightening of the defensive equipment, was lengthened

Indian infantryman equipped as an unarmoured spearman. (*Colour plate by Patricio Greve Moller, copyright of Gabriele Esposito*)

up to 3.6 metres. The new small shield could be strapped to the forearm, freeing the left hand to help hold the new longer type of spear. To sum up, Iphicrates made the panoply of the peltasts heavier and that of the hoplites lighter. Philip II of Macedonia adopted the equipment prescribed by the Athenian general for the new hoplites as the standard panoply of his phalangites, and thus the military reforms of Iphicrates had a very important impact on the development of the Macedonian army.

Egyptians

The Egyptians provided large numbers of marines to the Persians, as well as sizeable infantry units consisting of spearmen and archers. Most of the Egyptian soldiers were *machimoi*, professional hereditary warriors from the two warrior castes of the Hermotybies and the Kalasiries. These probably emerged during the Twenty-fifth Dynasty and comprised individuals who were forbidden to practice other activities outside of combat and were provided tax-free land as a reward for their military services. The Hermotybies came from Lower Egypt, while the Kalasiries came from Upper Egypt. The Persians, having a high opinion of the Egyptian warrior castes, always employed significant numbers of Egyptian infantrymen when there was no rebellion going on in Egypt. Both the marines and the infantrymen from Egypt were usually equipped as spearmen and wore cuirasses made from quilted linen. Several Egyptian foot soldiers carried massive body shields that were similar to the Assyrian ones and wore protective caps made of quilted linen. Egyptian marines and infantry both included sizeable numbers of archers, who often wore corselets made of brass scales.

Nubians, Ethiopians and Libyans

The Persians never exerted direct influence over the Nubian Kingdom of Kush (located south of Egypt) and the wild territory of Ethiopia. However, Achaemenid military forces often included contingents from these areas of Africa, which always had important links with Egypt. The Nubian auxiliaries were mostly equipped as archers, the bow being the 'national' weapon of the Kingdom of Kush. Nubian archers had fought for centuries in the armies of the pharaohs and were famed for their deadly precision. The Nubians from the Kingdom of Kush were called Ethiopians by the Persians despite not coming from Ethiopia. The 'true' Ethiopian warriors serving in the Achaemenid army consisted of archers or lightly equipped infantrymen armed with primitive studded clubs. They were well-known for their practice of painting their bodies half in red and half in white. Both the Nubians and the Ethiopians were

Indian cavalryman. Most Indian warriors were unarmoured but carried massive swords like the one shown here. (*Colour plate by Patricio Greve Moller, copyright of Gabriele Esposito*)

Indian archer. The bows used by the Indian foot troops were made of bamboo and were quite long, making them extremely powerful. (*Colour plate by Patricio Greve Moller, copyright of Gabriele Esposito*)

Indian infantryman (*left*) and archer (*right*).
(*Colour plate by Benedetto Esposito, copyright of Gabriele Esposito*)

usually cloaked in leopard and lion skins, while their effective bows were made of palm-wood strips that were 4 cubits long. The Libyan auxiliaries from the desert areas west of Egypt were only lightly armed, being equipped as tribal skirmishers with bows or throwing javelins.

Indians

Information is quite scarce on the Indian troops that were part of the Persian army. All that is available to reconstruct them is a couple of written sources: the *Arthasastra* and the *Mahabharata*. The *Arthasastra* is a manual on government and warfare attributed to a Maurya minister and dating to the years that followed Alexander the Great's invasion of India, while the *Mahabharata* is an epic poem from around 200 BC. Despite being written more than a century after the Macedonian invasion of India, the *Mahabharata* is full of interesting information for a modern reconstruction of the ancient Indian armies, because it describes Indian warfare of previous eras exactly like the *Iliad* (written around 800 BC) describes Mycenaean warfare of 1200 BC. Ancient Indian armies included four different categories of troops: infantry, cavalry, chariots and elephants. The infantry element was the most numerous, while chariots and elephants were the most prestigious. The *Mahabharata* gives proportions of one elephant to one chariot, three cavalrymen and five infantrymen. According to Arrian, the Indian army deployed at the Battle of the Hydaspes against Alexander the Great included 200 elephants, 420 chariots (each with a crew of six men), 6,000 cavalry and 30,000 infantry. While an impressive force for the standards of the time, it was not particularly so for an Indian army: around the same time, the Nanda Empire, the greatest state in India, could deploy an immense army with 3,000 elephants, 2,000 chariots, 20,000 cavalry and 200,000 infantry. From a tactical point of view, the infantry and cavalry had no active or significant roles on the battlefield, their main function being to protect the elephants and chariots by performing auxiliary duties. Each elephant or chariot was assigned a certain number of infantrymen and cavalrymen. Indian armies usually included contingents of mercenaries, fighting as archers or light infantrymen. The main difference between the tribal armies of northern India and those of the larger states located in the southern plains was in the number of elephants and chariots. Due to the geographical nature of their home territory, the northern tribes living in modern Pakistan had no chariots and very few elephants. With the notable exception of the nobles going to the battlefield on elephants or chariots, no Indian warriors wore any kind of personal protection. All the components of the army were lightly equipped: the cavalry was entirely made up of mounted javelineers, while the infantry included front-rank soldiers, javelineers and archers. The front-rank soldiers were armed with spears and tall body shields, but had no helmets or cuirasses. The foot javelineers, like the mounted ones, were equipped with smaller shields and javelins, making up the largest part of the infantry. The archers were the elite force of the Indian infantry, their tactical superiority being due to the excellence of their main weapon: heavy and powerful bamboo bows, 1.5 metres tall and having a hemp or sinew string that was drawn to the ear. Arrows were 3 cubits long, made of cane or reed and flighted with vulture feathers. Their heads were usually made of iron or horn. Sometimes these could be poisoned. The use of poisoned arrows was apparently forbidden during the wars fought between Indian states, but they were employed against foreign invaders. Kings and nobles, fighting on elephants or chariots, were armed with javelins or spears and were protected by brass helmets and very simple scale armour. As secondary weapons, the Indian warriors had massive swords and maces or clubs. The swords had a broad blade that was 3 cubits in length and were used to deliver powerful two-handed cutting blows, brought down from above the head. Maces and clubs could be used in one hand, two hands or thrown; according to ancient sources, Indian fighters were very good at using these primitive but effective weapons. Ancient Indian armies were thus large forces of lightly equipped infantry that comprised elite contingents of charioteers and archers, plus the devastating shock force represented by the elephant corps.

Bibliography

Primary Sources

Arrian, *Anabasis of Alexander*
Arrian, *Indike*
Arrian, *Tactics*
Asklepiodotos, *Tactics*
Diodorus Siculus, *History*
Herodotus, *The Histories*
Plutarch, *Lives*
Polybius, *The Histories*
Quintus Curtius, *History of Alexander*
Strabo, *Geography*
Thucydides, *History of the Peloponnesian War*
Xenophon, *Anabasis*
Xenophon, *Hellenica*
Xenophon, *Kyropaidia*
Xenophon, *On Horsemanship*
Xenophon, *The Cavalry Commander*

Secondary Sources

Anderson, E.B., *Cataphracts: Knights of the Ancient Eastern Empires* (Pen & Sword, 2016).
Cassin, Scott J., *The Greek and Persian Wars 500–323 BC* (Osprey Publishing, 1977).
Cernenko, E.V., *The Scythians 700–300 BC* (Osprey Publishing, 1983).
Connolly, P., *Greece and Rome at War* (MacDonald, 1981).
Everson, T., *Warfare in Ancient Greece: Arms and Armour from the Heroes of Homer to Alexander the Great* (The History Press, 2005).
Gorelik, K., *Warriors of Eurasia* (Montvert Publishing, 1995).
Head, D., *Armies of the Macedonian and Punic Wars* (Wargames Research Group, 1982).
Head, D., *The Achaemenid Persian Army* (Montvert Publishing, 1992).
Karasulas, A., *Mounted Archers of the Steppe 600 BC–AD 1300* (Osprey Publishing, 2004).
Nelson, R., *Armies of the Greek and Persian Wars* (Wargames Research Group, 1978).
Nikorov, V.P., *The Armies of Bactria 700 BC–450 AD* (Montvert Publishing, 1997).
Quesada Sanz, F., *Armas de Grecia y Roma* (La Esfera, 2014).
Sage, M., *Warfare in Ancient Greece: A Sourcebook* (Psychology Press, 1996).
Sekunda, N., *The Army of Alexander the Great* (Osprey Publishing, 1984).
Sekunda, N., *The Persian Army 560–330 BC* (Osprey Publishing, 1992).
Warry, J., *Warfare in the Classical World* (Salamander Books, 1997).
Webber, C., *The Thracians 700 BC–AD 46* (Osprey Publishing, 2001).

The Re-enactors who Contributed to this Book

Make Carthage Great Again

Make Carthage Great Again is a Facebook page run by a small group of living history enthusiasts. The group began its activity in January 2022. The purpose of the page is to highlight the Punic/Carthaginian civilization through articles, photographs and information in order to underline the superior qualities of this peculiar civilization. The group is based in France and works on the reconstruction of military life as well as of the Carthaginians' everyday life. The work of the group is based on available archaeological sources and is aimed at highlighting Carthaginian culture through civil and military historical reconstructions. Their photography is made as realistic as possible by working with great accuracy on the sets and landscapes and by focusing on the costumes that are reconstructed according to written primary sources.

Make Carthage Great Again est une page Facebook tenue par un petit groupe de passionnés d'histoire vivante. Le groupe commence son activité en janvier 2022. Le but de cette page est de mettre en avant la civilisation carthaginoise/punique par le biais d'articles, de photos et d'information mettant en avant la qualité de cette civilisation si particulière. Le groupe, basé en France, travaille autant sur la reconstitution de la vie de tous les jours que sur la partie militaire. Le travail est basé sur les sources archéologiques disponibles et la mise en avant de la culture carthaginoise par la reconstitution historique civile et militaire. Leur photographie se veut le plus réaliste possible, travaillant sur les décors et paysage pour mettre en avant le travail sur les costumes et sur les textes.

Contacts:
E-mail: denistaverne@hotmail.com
Facebook: https://www.facebook.com/profile.php?id=100077371074336&mibextid=LQQJ4d

Ancient Thrace

The living history association Ancient Thrace was created in 2015 as historical re-enactment group by enthusiasts from Yambol in Bulgaria, who were fascinated by the ancient history of their land and wanted to express their passion for it. The association now has around twenty permanent members and many 'friends' coming from different places who often join its activities. The efforts of the group have as their main aim that of reconstructing the lifestyle, culture and military equipment of the Thracian tribes in the period 400 BC–AD 100. With the progression of time, they also started to reconstruct other peoples living in the Balkans during Antiquity: Celts (300 BC–AD 100), Germani (AD 100–200) and Goths (AD 300–400). In their activities and reconstructions, they try to be as historically accurate as they can. Their equipment is based on countless hours of interpreting ancient documents and archaeological evidences; their process of research and experimentation never stops. During recent years, they have participated successfully in several festivals in Bulgaria and abroad, and have also collaborated in the creation of movies and books. All these positive experiences have increased their confidence and stimulated the general improvement of the group. Since the Ancient Thrace group was created, its members have visited amazing destinations and met great people, learned more about history and shared superb memories together. For them, historical re-enactment is a special passion that combines an interest with history with their desire to learn more about the past. Members wish to reach people and share with them the emotions of this passion, which has become a very important component of their daily life.

Contacts:
Facebook: https://www.facebook.com/AncientThrace/

Amages Drachen

Amages Drachen is a re-enactment group created by means of Living History i.e. through reconstructions of clothing and artefacts, to make history more tangible. Members come from the Rhine-Main and Stuttgart areas and are committed to teaching and depicting ancient steppe cultures. Both Scythian and Sarmatian representations from the period of about 600 BC to approximately AD 300, which members have produced on the basis of archaeological finds and historical sources, are part of their repertoire. The group like to introduce event visitors to the material culture of ancient steppe nomads with self-created replicas, explanations and lectures. The steppe belt today includes large parts of Ukraine, Russia, Kazakhstan, Kyrgyzstan and Mongolia, and was inhabited in ancient times by nomadic tribes such as the

Scythians, Saka, Sauromatians and Sarmatians, who are also part of the group's representations. Unfortunately, these nomadic cultures have left no written records of themselves. The knowledge of these scripture-free cultures can today only be taken from archaeological finds and written sources of neighbouring cultures. From the first millennium BC until late Antiquity, these ancient nomads stood in constant contact with the settled 'high cultures' on the edge of the steppe belt: Persians, Chinese, Greeks and Romans. These cultural contacts were both peaceful and warlike: on the one hand, the nomads benefited from the trade routes through the steppe areas (the Silk Road); on the other, the mounted archers were dreaded warriors and coveted mercenaries. Despite this, these 'mer-milkers' and 'horse-bowers', as they were called by ancient authors, are still rarely found in the current knowledge of history, but they have always had a decisive influence on European history and have contributed to shape the present-day face of Europe.

Contacts:
E-mail: amages.drachen@gmx.de
Website: https://www.sarmaten-steppenkultur.de/index.php/en/home-3/

Index